The

Your Heart

Freedom to live the life of your dreams through Network Marketing

Kathy Paauw

CONTENTS

DEDICATION

To my husband, Doug, and my daughter, Carly, without whom this book would not have been written. You have been my most important teachers. Your unconditional love has helped me learn many of the life lessons I share in this book. Your encouragement has given me the courage to pursue what makes my heart sing.

This book is also dedicated to you, the reader, for embracing knowledge to advance your personal and professional development. I celebrate your commitment to being the best you can be as you learn to sing the music of your heart!

The world would have us believe that if we want to receive financial abundance and become financially free, we have to work really hard and get a lucky break. Those who have been involved in network marketing know otherwise. Success is not about getting lucky but about taking full responsibility for our thoughts, our actions, and the results they produce. It's also about duplicating what other successful network marketing professionals have taught us.

Kathy Paauw is one of the most successful productivity coaches I know, and she is also a highly successful network marketing professional. This book is worth its weight in gold. Kathy shares some powerful tools that will enable any network marketing professional to build a successful business. I love her passion for helping others achieve financial and lifestyle freedom while tapping into their own gifts and talents in a way that makes their heart sing.

I first met Kathy in 2007 when I was a keynote speaker at a conference she attended. Later that year, she attended my basic and advanced Breakthrough to Success trainings. I really got to know her better when she participated in my Platinum Inner Circle year-long program in 2008. As a result, I invited Kathy to be a guest presenter on my monthly expert call for our Platinum Mastermind group, and we all received great value from her.

Later that year, I invited Kathy to come work with me in my office to help me learn how to better manage paper and information flow. She taught me a simple but powerful process that has helped me make better decisions in my life with paper, e-mail, voice mail, verbal requests from others, and all the thoughts in my head about things I need to do. Using the process I learned from Kathy has given me peace of mind, knowing that I have a plan to handle what's most important. She'll teach you the same process in this book.

Network marketing has been in existence for more than fifty years, and it is finally earning the respect that it deserves. Today it is considered to be the best business model around for creating financial freedom and lifestyle freedom. It is the great equalizer—empowering anyone from anywhere, with any educational background, and with any social, ethnic, and financial heritage—to build a thriving business. The only limitation is how big one can dream.

Because I am such a believer in network marketing, we published *Chicken Soup for the Network Marketer's Soul*; the quality, depth, and variety of stories we collected made us laugh, cry, and get goose bumps. We were totally inspired by the stories of people who had gone for and achieved their dreams—all through the vehicle of network marketing.

Network marketing is much more than a business model. It is a way of life. Those who get deeply involved in building a network marketing business undergo one of the most rewarding and challenging personal development experiences they'll ever have. As the business grows, one learns that there are no limits on us except the ones we impose on ourselves. That's why the emphasis on personal development is so important.

I am excited that you have chosen to read Kathy's book, and I encourage you to complete the Freedom Challenges she provides at the end of each chapter. These exercises will help you plug into your own creative genius and untapped potential so you can live the life of your dreams while building a thriving network marketing business.

—Jack Canfield
Creator of the *Chicken Soup for the Soul*® series
Coauthor of *The Success Principles*™:
How to Get from Where You Are to Where You Want to Be

 KATHY PAAUW

Kathy's book is the right message at the right time! You get the blueprint for better living from one of the best pros in network marketing, along with wisdom that will inspire and improve your life for the better. If you don't read and pick up several nuggets of wisdom contained in this book, I'd be shocked. When someone shares their wisdom, talents and treasures in the pages of a book, it's the biggest bargain on the planet. Get this book NOW and let it capture both your heart and mind!

—Tony Rubleski
Best-selling author of the *Mind Capture* series
www.MindCaptureBook.com

Kathy has compiled the perfect balance of information and inspiration, combined it with easy-to-complete exercises, and rolled it all into one compact book which gives the foundation needed to build a successful network marketing business. *The Music of Your Heart* is a fantastic resource for any network marketing professional wanting to "find the music of their heart" and then learn the hands-on tools needed to support that dream.

—Dana Wilde
Author of *Train Your Brain*
Host of the Mind Aware Teleseminar for Network Marketers

Kathy's book offers an insightful look at the needs of people in the world of network marketing. She demonstrates a profound knowledge of the profession and does a superlative job teaching both the "inner" and "outer" skills necessary to excel in the field. I especially like Kathy's use of stories and metaphors for making an occasionally difficult subject easier to grasp, and her useful and user-friendly exercises. In my experience, the combination of a clear step-by-step system, combined with the use of stories, quotes, and exercises are the ingredients that propel a book to number one bestseller status. I have no doubt that Kathy's practical yet uplifting approach will propel her quickly to similar heights.

—Dr. Steve Taubman
Author of the #1 bestseller
UnHypnosis for Direct Sellers, Network Marketers, and Entrepreneurs
www.stevetaubman.com

                KATHY PAAUW

The Music of Your Heart is a must-read book for all network marketers! Kathy Paauw combines her skills as an experienced network marketing professional and a trained coach to give you the tools to address the most common challenges network marketers face today. She outlines the ultimate blueprint to build a successful network marketing business for you and your entire team.

—Ivan Misner
NY Times Bestselling author
Founder of BNI® and Referral Institute®

The Music of Your Heart has changed my life. It is simple in presentation, but profound in meaning. It is a book dedicated to an action plan that is sure to have dramatic improvement for those willing to follow the basic steps. Its message on accountability—not only to another person, but more importantly to oneself—is so on target. For all who read this, the secret of being emotionally and spiritually wealthy will be there for the taking. This book offers such a simple and attainable plan. After doing several of the exercises, amazing things have happened. For the first time, I felt the burnout I created for myself disappear. I am already applying what I've learned, not only to my life, but to my network marketing business. Thank you for letting me hear the music of my heart.

—Philip Mongelluzzo, MD
Board Certified Internist
Network Marketing Entrepreneur

This book is a mindful, heartful masterpiece . . . a combination of common sense and brilliance balanced with a blend of passionate giving and meaningful insight. You will not only be inspired by this piece of art, but changed for good, for life. Whether a lover of music or just one who appreciates the talents of others, this will not only be easy to read and understand, but applicable immediately to your mind, heart and spirit.

—Jennifer M. Leeds
Director of Sales and Marketing
Tupperware Brands

Kathy has created a very important book for our times. The information she has brought together from so many great sources is invaluable and not just for the network marketing profession, but also for the average person who is struggling to organize their lives, their careers and their futures! For us, this book is just as important as Kiyosaki's *The Business of the 21st Century*. Every one of our distributors, as well as our family members, will receive a copy of *The Music of Your Heart*.

—Kenton and Ricky Pass
Business Owners
Network Marketing Entrepreneurs

The Music of Your Heart is stunning! What a fabulous compendium of good wisdom, tools, tips, information, examples, stories, and quotes—the best of the best all in one handy little guidebook for entrepreneurial success. I was particularly tickled with the "Freedom Challenges." Bravo!

—Fran Fisher
Master Certified Coach, FJFisher Coaching and Consulting
Network Marketing Entrepreneur

Kathy's book is a terrific compilation of contemporary leadership thinking laced with exercises and examples applicable in the network marketing world. The "Freedom Challenge" exercises are simple, yet profound. *The Music of Your Heart* will challenge and delight its readers.

—Dana Phillips
Associate Certified Coach
Direct Selling Coach and Partner, Team Connections

Kathy Paauw delivers a solid game plan for what it takes to create the mindset, organization and the personal development path that is critical to your success in Network Marketing. Follow her guide, take the necessary actions and you will have success in your business.

—Jackie Ulmer
Network Marketing Professional and Trainer

 KATHY PAAUW

If you are tired of living paycheck to paycheck and are ready to be successful in network marketing, then you have to read Kathy's book first! She gives a very clear and concise road map for what it takes to be successful, not only in business but in life. Kathy shows you how to create a life, not just make a living. Her book was music to my brain and now I can sing success! Thank you, Kathy.

—Tim R. Green
Author of *Set 4 Life*
Referral Marketing Expert
www.RIofMI.com

If you combine the tools in this book with a passion for the company you are with and massive action, you can't help but become successful.

—Mike Dolpies
Author of *Motion Before Motivation, The Success Secret That Never Fails*

The Music of Your Heart is not only a fantastic blueprint for success in life and business, it compels you to interpret your desires, dreams, and ambitions into a real action plan. Kathy does a brilliant job of sharing success principles that have helped many people achieve their dream of creating true freedom in their lives. Kathy reminds us that we are the conductors in our orchestra of life, and can create it in any way we desire!

—Dave "The Shef" Sheffield
Top business motivational speaker and author of five top selling books
www.theshef.com

Thinking in the abstract, and with the wisdom and experience of an old master, through her conversational tone, stories, and Freedom Challenge exercises, Kathy has created the Why and How of giving your *intention . . . attention . . .* to help you succeed in your direct sales business. Whether you are new to direct selling or an experienced top producer, *The Music of Your Heart* is a must-read.

—Linda D. Lucas
Direct Selling Executive, Business Consultant, Speaker and Trainer
www.lindalucas.com

The Music of Your Heart is an easy and enjoyable read. The "Freedom Challenges" are simple to follow, yet create powerful results. If you want a tool that will pave your pathway to success in network marketing, this is it.

—Terra Larsen
Co-Author of *Build It Big*
Top Direct Sales Earner
Certified Business Coach
Certified Elite Leader

Wow, this book is awesome and I could not put it down once I started reading it. I have just sucked up every word and have had many light bulb moments in just a couple of short hours. The Freedom Challenges are just what I needed. Before, I seemed to not know what I didn't know. Now I know where to focus and I am thinking in a whole new direction. Thank you, Kathy, for sharing your story, your insights, your love and your encouragement. You are a precious gift, especially to this girl on the other side of the world. You are changing lives in ways that you cannot even imagine. I know your book will take thousands of people to a whole new level in their personal and professional lives, as it has done for me.

—Tarnya Hawkins
Network Marketing Entrepreneur

The Music of Your Heart offers a unique combination of sage advice for those just getting started in direct sales, as well as coaching tools for anyone who wishes to be mentored by a master. Kathy also shares some productivity tools that will help you run a more effective business. Her Freedom Challenges at the end of each chapter are skillfully designed to help you tap into what makes your heart sing, anchor your learning, and create an action plan for success in life and business.

—Nicki Keohohou, CEO and Co-founder
Direct Selling Women's Alliance
www.dswa.org

IN GRATITUDE

Gratitude is the memory of the heart.

—French proverb

I deeply appreciate all the support I have received from family, friends, mentors, colleagues, and team members. It is impossible to mention everyone who has contributed to my life and has helped make this book a reality, and it is appropriate to mention a few.

My heartfelt appreciation to . . .

Dad for encouraging me to sing and for teaching me some powerful lessons, in life and in death; **Mom** for your enthusiasm and encouragement; **Mom and Dad Paauw** for your unconditional love and support and for the gift of your amazing son; **Jo Lynne Pelletier** for being a wonderful sister, friend, and a great support; **Phil Wells** for teaching me life lessons even when you didn't know you were; **Jack Canfield** for being my most influential mentor and for teaching me to love myself; **Stephen Covey** for providing powerful tools that have helped me put first things first; **Jim Bunch** for teaching me how to balance my life between happiness, health, and wealth creation; **Hale Dwoskin** for teaching me how to "let go" and embrace what is; **Thomas Leonard** for the gift of the nine environments model and many other powerful coaching tools; **Robert MacPhee** for helping me learn how to manifest my intentions; **Kody Bateman** for sharing your vision, for encouraging me to dream bigger and focus on the positive, and for providing a pathway for millions of people to change the world; **Jodi Bateman** for your unconditional love, kindness, and for supporting Kody through the start-up challenges; **Jordan Adler** for teaching me how to be a true servant leader and for being such an amazing mentor; **Judy O'Higgins** for your consistent mentoring, support, encouragement, and friendship; **Kate Harper** for sharing with me one of the greatest opportunities of a lifetime; **Michele Reynolds** for your virtual support and for loving and affirming me when I need it; **Barbara Hemphill** for teaching me much of what I now teach others about working more productively; **Chris Crouch** for teaching me your paper and information management process and so much more; **Fran Fisher**

for your incredible coach training and for helping me discover my core purpose in life; **BJ Levy** for being my coach, mentor, and friend through all the ups and downs of my life; **Debbie Gilster** for being my accountability partner, friend, and mentor; **Liz Garza** for your unconditional love, encouragement, honest feedback, and for being my friend; **Mary Miller** for your encouragement and help in fine-tuning my book with your editorial comments; **Daniel Barrozo** at the Ink Studio for creating my book cover; **Kevin Cole** for composing the music and recording it with me, and for longtime friendship and support over the past 34 years; **Fabsound Records** for recording the song; **my many team members, mentors, colleagues, and corporate staff I work with daily**, who so freely share ideas that move our profession forward, and from whom I have learned so much. You are my family and I love and cherish you all. I honor and thank you for being my teacher, my friend, my cheerleader, my mirror, and my supporter as I've learned how to sing my own song. My deepest gratitude goes to **my loving Creator** for blessings beyond measure. I am humbly grateful for the gifts and talents that allow me to step forward and fulfill my deepest desire: to be a messenger of peace, balance, and harmony.

In honor and in memory of those who have supported me on my path to freedom, I am donating the proceeds of this book to **World Vision**. For more information, visit *www.WorldVision.org*. They do an incredible job of helping people gain freedom by leveraging resources.

INTRODUCTION

Why do people start a network marketing business? Many say it's because they want *freedom* to do what they want to do, when they want to do it, with whom they want to do it, and where and how they want to do it.

Unfortunately, some of the home-based business owners I know—including network marketing professionals—are among the most captive people I've ever met. They have become prisoners of their own walls with a tyrant of a boss who cracks the whip much harder than any previous employer ever did. They have a belief that if they just "work a little harder," they will be successful. The road to financial freedom can take its toll on your lifestyle if you fall prey to some of the traps common to many business owners.

To understand these traps, it's important to recognize that wealth is not just about the paychecks you receive for your efforts. Achieving true financial freedom includes much more than the external wealth accumulating in your bank account. Wealth from within includes peace, joy, love, satisfaction, safety, and well-being.

True *financial freedom* contributes to a greater sense of overall freedom—being able to enjoy and live life on your own terms and having the peace of mind and the satisfaction of being able to experience the *lifestyle freedom* that financial freedom can provide. I have written this book for all network marketing professionals, whether you are just getting started or have been running your business for years, whether you are building your business on a part-time basis or this is your primary business.

Please note that throughout this book I will refer to our profession as *network marketing*. Other common terms include *multi-level marketing (MLM)* and *direct selling*. Although distinctions can be made between these business models, the ideas and suggestions provided in this book can be equally applied, regardless of which term you use to describe your business.

In this book, I'll share some tools that have been indispensable in creating my own financial and lifestyle freedom. My wish for you is that the contents of this book will help you begin to enjoy some lifestyle freedom right now—regardless of your current financial circumstances—while enjoying the journey along the way to financial freedom and finding a path that makes your heart sing.

I have been a home-based business owner since 1995. By my seventh year, I had built a thriving coaching and consulting practice. Even with a full client load, I was not generating the kind of income I desired. Although I was passionate about what I was doing, I was working long hours and my life was completely out of balance. As a life coach, I felt like a real hypocrite helping others to better balance their lives when my own was so out of whack. The only way I knew how to generate more income was to work harder even though I was already working long hours. I woke up one day and realized that I did not really own my own business—it owned me!

In 2002, I was first introduced to the concept of leverage—something I later learned was a core success ingredient for what we do as network marketers. I realized that leveraging my time through the efforts of others was what it would take to increase my income because I was not willing to work any harder, especially at the expense of my health and relationships. I had started down the path of leveraging my time by offering group coaching and consulting and marketing some recorded workshops, but I still was not generating the kind of income I desired, and I was working way too many hours.

In 2005, a friend introduced me to a network marketing company that was a perfect fit for me. I fell in love with the company's products, culture, values, and the people it attracted. I was so excited about it that I became a distributor and naturally started sharing the company's offerings with the people I knew. My network marketing business took off like a rocket. I received my first promotion in two months and my second promotion after only four months with the company.

I decided to build my network marketing business on the side while I continued to run my other business. By 2007, I realized that I was generating more income from my part-time network marketing business than I was from my thriving twelve-year-old full-time coaching and consulting business. At this point, it was hard for me to ignore the fact that I was trading time for dollars in my service business while leveraging my time through the efforts of others in my network marketing business. By the end of 2007, I had 1,500 distributors on my team. I had personally sponsored only fifty-seven of them (less than 4

 KATHY PAAUW

percent) in the twenty-seven months I had been in business, and I was one of the top income earners in my company.

It doesn't take a rocket scientist to figure out which business had the greatest leveraging power and return on my time investment!

Trying to run both businesses separately was taking its toll on me. I was spending most of my waking hours in my home office. I had gained weight, I was stressed out, and my lack of free time was also affecting my relationships. I had convinced myself that I did not have time to go to the gym or take an evening off to just "hang out" with my family.

One of the reasons I was originally attracted to the network marketing model was because I wanted to leverage my time so I could enjoy financial *and* lifestyle freedom. I knew something had to change, but I loved my coaching and consulting work and did not want to give it up.

In February of 2009, I took a two-week vacation with my family to Australia and New Zealand. I had not checked e-mail for more than a week, and something was nagging at me to log in. As I quickly scrolled past over a thousand e-mail messages that had accumulated, one in particular caught my attention. It was an e-mail from a colleague of mine, revealing some news that I thought would have a huge negative impact on the consulting side of my business. I felt like twelve years of my work was crumbling before my eyes. I was so upset by the news that I did not sleep more than an hour that night.

The next morning, I was watching some local headline news reports about several devastating wildfires that were raging near Melbourne. I remember feeling like my business back home was burning up too.

Then I had a thought that changed everything.

Sometimes forestry experts will start a fire on purpose so they can burn down the overgrowth and make room for new shoots to sprout.

My business back home *was* burning up, and suddenly I felt completely at peace with everything. I had just received a huge gift, and I knew exactly what to do next.

When I returned home from vacation, I posted a notice on my website that I was not taking any new coaching or consulting clients. Because I love coaching and supporting people to achieve their goals, I decided to incorporate this work into my network marketing business.

Since then, I have *given away* my coaching and consulting services to team members who are serious about creating financial and lifestyle freedom for themselves and others. Investing in my team in this way has enabled me to inspire and guide others to share their gifts of greatness, and that has promoted team growth. I love having the freedom to design my business and my life in a way that makes my heart sing and helps others to do the same!

Each of us has been given a combination of unique gifts that nobody else on earth was created with. What are your special gifts? I invite you to find out who you are and give yourself away! In other words, listen to and follow the music of your heart. You'll experience a lot more joy and success when you contribute to the world in a way that is authentic to you.

I felt compelled to write this book because of some observations I have made since becoming a network marketing professional. Many of the people entering our profession today have never been their own boss. Starting your own business can feel intimidating and sometimes even overwhelming. The tools provided in this book are designed to help you live a balanced, fulfilling, and productive life as you begin or continue your journey to achieve financial freedom or whatever it is that you desire.

This book contains four sections. The first section provides tools to help you dig deep and get clear about your intentions and your bigger *why* for starting your business. This foundational work is critical to network marketers because there will be times that you feel discouraged or you feel like quitting. Your bigger *why* for doing this work will keep you motivated to continue, no matter what challenges you encounter.

The second section provides tools to help you identify where your personal and work life is off balance by looking at nine distinct areas of your life. Striking a balance is critical to success in both your work life and your personal life. Once you are aware of imbalances, you can "upgrade" these areas to support the ultimate lifestyle freedom you desire.

The third section will help you work more productively. You will find tools to help you clarify your priorities and then plan and manage how you invest your time and resources in your network marketing business. As the CEO of your own company (yes, you are the CEO!), you don't have anyone holding you accountable, telling you what to do or when and how to do it. I'll share some tools that many other CEOs have used to help them run multimillion dollar companies.

The fourth section provides a review of the suggested "Freedom Challenges" or exercises provided at the end of each chapter, which are designed to help you clarify, create, and support your path to freedom so you can be successful in building your network marketing business, live the life of your dreams, and help others do the same.

Each chapter includes personal stories that illustrate some of the core concepts and tools that have enabled me to move from being captive to being free. As you read this book and do the Freedom Challenges at the end of each chapter, I hope your outer journey will align with your heart's desires—the music of your heart—so you feel on purpose and with purpose.

One thing I know: the only ones among you who will be really happy
are those who have sought and found how to serve.

—Albert Schweitzer

PART ONE

Clarify Your Path to Freedom

Why Network Marketing?

Network marketing is the most giving form of business model in existence. Giving the gift of freedom, the gift of employment and the gift of a future opportunity is the greatest gift ever. I believe network marketing is the key to solving the economic problems of our time.

—Mark Victor Hansen

We live in interesting times. With six billion people on our planet, there simply are not enough traditional jobs for everyone who wants to be gainfully employed. Technology has changed the face of the way we do business. As more people become educated and employable, there are fewer traditional jobs to be found. People around the globe are ready to embrace what network marketing has to offer.

Here are several reasons why I believe that right now is the best time to be part of the network marketing profession:

- Although network marketing was born in the 1950s, the mainstream has not embraced this business model until recently. We are seeing people from all walks of life joining network marketing companies and promoting this business model.

- Network marketing enables people to do part-time work and receive full-time pay and lifetime benefits.

- Because baby boomers started reaching retirement age in 2011—an estimated seventy-eight million baby boomers turning sixty-five over the next twenty years in the United States alone—a staggering number of retirement-age people are excited about network marketing opportunities. Many of them have lost retirement funds in the stock market crash and are highly motivated to work from home.

- College graduates are finding that a degree does not guarantee them a job. In addition, our emerging generation has seen what the "corporate" model has done to their parents, and many of them do not want to follow in their parents' footsteps. Lifestyle freedom is of high importance to this generation. No special education or previous network marketing experience is necessary to do well. They love being able to pursue their passions while building residual income on the side.

- When the economy is in a recession and unemployment is high, network marketing companies experience exponential growth. Bad economic news for most people is good economic news for network marketers.

- Many countries around the world have unstable economies, and our profession offers global financial solutions.

- In today's economy, people don't have access to the hundreds of thousands of dollars necessary to start a traditional business. Because start-up costs are so low for network marketing businesses, there is essentially no barrier to entry. If someone really wants to get started, they will find a way to manifest the resources necessary to do so, which in most cases is under $500. Network marketing allows you to be in business without taking on the typical financial risks associated with starting your own business.

People starting a traditional business or a franchise have done their homework and know that they will have high start-up costs and will also require other means of support for at least two years. They are also prepared to work extra hard those first couple of years even though their take-home pay is zero. In network marketing, we are fortunate to have low start-up costs, and we can work part-time to achieve business growth as long as we work consistently.

Many network marketing professionals are not prepared for the fact that business start-ups don't usually generate an immediate profit. It's unfortunate that network marketing has been tainted with get-rich-quick promises made by a small number of people in our profession. Making any income claims—perceived or real—is something that can get us in trouble. In the United States, the Federal

Trade Commission (FTC) can shut a company down if their distributors share income claims with prospects, as these claims often set unrealistic expectations for people getting started. When expectations and reality don't match, many new distributors will quit.

I have observed something in common with many distributors who struggle to build their business. Although they may be consistently doing the right things, they are not successfully building a team. This is often because they feel desperate to sell products and sign up distributors. Even if they don't think they are acting like a desperate person, their desperation is conveyed to their prospects. Desperation kills opportunity.

One of the first questions I ask a new distributor is this: *do you need immediate income in order to take care of basic needs for yourself and your dependents?* If they say yes, I encourage them to get a job as soon as possible or keep the job they already have. Why? Expecting your network marketing business to instantly generate income to cover all your basic needs will put huge pressure on you to "perform" at a certain level. That pressure turns into desperation. Prospects will run the opposite direction when they sense desperation. It's your responsibility to take care of your basic needs so you don't become one of those "desperate" distributors.

Starting a network marketing business is not a get-rich-quick venture. You may hear about someone who rapidly built a large team that generates a livable income for themselves in just a few months. Usually, such individuals have spent years building a network of people who know, like, and trust them; and they were able to quickly sponsor some friends and colleagues and get them excited about building a business. If you have already invested years of your life building a solid network, you may be able to escalate the speed of your team growth.

The vast majority of network marketers need to cultivate the soil, plant some seeds, water, and fertilize before they can reap the harvest. When done consistently on a part-time basis, working ten to fifteen hours a week, it typically takes two to five years to build a team that will generate a solid residual lifetime income. If you want to grow faster, you need to consistently invest more hours each week.

I've found that most novice network marketers do not understand the basic factors that contribute to their success, so they give up early in their business development. Then they join the chorus of former network marketers who sing the song, "MLMs never work . . . only a few people at the top make any money." Some will blame the multi-level marketing company and start working with a different company, only to experience the same results again.

Some people have joined several network marketing companies over time, hoping to achieve financial freedom with each one. Usually, they blame the previous companies they were with. They have not figured out that the common denominator in their failures is them. When I hear a "serial network marketer" say that they will *try* what I am offering, I tell them that I would rather they not invest anything to get started as a business builder unless they are ready to make a two-to-five-year commitment to doing so. Would someone invest $250,000+ in a franchise just to *try* it? Probably not! Too often I see people who don't take their business seriously, and then they wonder why it never took off.

Here are eight important factors for success in network marketing:

1. The company you choose needs to be the *right fit for you*. Are you passionate about what you have to offer, either because of the product or because of the offer itself? If not, find a company that is a better fit. Your passion will carry you through the tough times.

2. Be clear about your *financial goals*. Do you just want to pay for your own product usage? Do you want to generate a few hundred dollars extra each month? Or do you want to generate lifetime residual income that will enable you to enjoy financial and lifestyle freedom?

   Although you do not need to fully understand your company's compensation plan, be sure that the plan meets your needs. If your goal is to eventually retire and live off residual pay (income that comes in whether you work or not), be sure that the compensation plan is designed to provide that for you.

3. Create a *culture and a community with attributes and values that attract others*: integrity, authenticity, encouragement, recognition, empowerment, generosity, respect, kindness, friendship, and fun.

4. Be clear about *why business success is important to you*. What is your bigger *why* for doing this?

 KATHY PAAUW

5. Be a *student of personal development*. Your own belief system provides the foundation upon which your business will either grow and thrive or fail. Build a solid foundation that will support solid growth. Let go of limiting beliefs and learn how to get out of your own way and believe in yourself.

   In *The Slight Edge*, Jeff Olson says this: "The greatest gift you could ever give yourself is also the wisest business investment you could ever make. It is also the most critical step in accomplishing any challenging task, and is the one step without which all other success strategies, no matter how brilliant or time-tested, are doomed to fail. What is this mysterious gift? It is your own personal development. Investing in your own improvement, your own personal growth and betterment, is all these things and more."

6. *Be disciplined.* All good network marketing companies offer a simple process that can be duplicated. When you create duplication, you also create passive income. Discipline yourself to do the right activities consistently over time, and teach others to do the same. Do what you are committed to do, whether you feel like it or not.

7. *Never quit on a bad day.* Because network marketing professionals have less "skin in the game" than a traditional business owner, it is much easier for some to quit when they encounter disappointments. As Jim Rohn once said, "discipline your disappointments."

   In Kody Bateman's book, *MLM Blueprint* (available in 2012), he calls these disappointments "shutdowns." There are three common shutdowns that all network marketers eventually experience:

   - *Shutdown #1*: People you are certain will be your best prospects may disappoint you when they have no interest in what you have to offer. Family and friends may tell you that what you're doing is a scam and you should have nothing to do with it.

   - *Shutdown #2*: You are certain that a new team member you just sponsored is going to be a big business builder. This new distributor is very excited and talks about plans to build a huge team. Suddenly your new team member quits coming to events and won't return your phone calls. You have no idea why he/she has dropped off the face of the earth. Chances are, this team member has experienced shutdown #1 and was not prepared for it.

- *Shutdown #3*: You will hit plateaus as you build your team. A plateau is when your team has been consistently growing, and suddenly your growth curve goes flat or even takes a dip. Although your team is bringing on new distributors, it is also losing some due to attrition from inactive distributors who decide not to renew. This happens to everyone, no matter what company you are with and how long you have been in business.

All three of these are normal and predictable in our profession. Those who understand the law of averages are more likely to work through these shutdowns. Those who are not prepared for these inevitable experiences may quit. It has been said that "you can learn a lot about the size of a man by knowing the size of the problem that brought him down."

8. *Be responsible and do whatever is necessary to take care of your basic needs* while you are building your business, so desperation does not creep in. Desperation kills opportunity.

I want to emphasize this last point. You may dislike your current job, or you may currently be unemployed. Free yourself from the deadly emotional bind of feeling desperate by doing whatever is necessary to take care of your basic needs while building your network marketing business over the next several years.

If you love your work and you want to continue with it, great! Many people in network marketing work part-time on their business while doing other work they love. A friend of mine loves his performance career, but the gigs are sporadic, and there's no security in his work as a musician. For a long time, he lived "on the edge" because if he did not perform, he did not get paid. He is passionate about his work as a musician, and he also needs consistent income. In just four years, he has been able to grow his part-time network marketing business to a level that generates two times the income he earns as a musician. His network marketing business offers him the flexibility he needs with his schedule while supporting the lifestyle he desires. He has also created residual income so he can comfortably retire—not something he could have done before as a musician.

For those who do not enjoy your current work, you may wonder how soon you can quit your job. Network marketing is designed to be worked as a part-time business until you get it going. I suggest that you remain gainfully employed until you can meet all four of these conditions:

1. You are covering your business expenses, including your own product purchase, personal development costs, and travel to team and company events.
2. For at least six consecutive months, you have generated enough income from your network marketing business to meet the basic needs of you and your dependents. (Your network marketing income may be combined with reliable income earned by other members of your household to meet your family budget.)
3. You have paid off all debt (exception: affordable mortgage on your home).
4. You have enough cash reserves to support you and your dependents for at least six months in the event that something unforeseen happened.

Without all four of these conditions in place, you could be setting yourself up for financial disaster. If I sound like a broken record, it's because this point is so critical to your success in network marketing. *Avoid creating an environment where you feel desperate since desperation becomes deadly when you want to build something!*

For my first three and a half years, I worked my network marketing business alongside my business that was paying the bills until such time that I no longer relied on my other income and I was able to meet all the conditions listed above. Building my team from a place of abundance rather than desperation has made it so much easier to grow since my prospects' decisions did not determine my financial health.

FREEDOM CHALLENGE

Whether you are brand-new to network marketing or you've been in business for a while, I suggest that you do these exercises unless you have already done this.

1. Create a realistic budget for your business expenses:

   - Product purchase
   - Personal development (books, CDs, workshops, etc.)
   - Team and company meetings/trainings (including travel costs)
   - Administrative support (bookkeeper, virtual assistant, etc.)
   - Office expenses (telephone, computer, supplies, etc.)
   - Marketing support (website, Internet, collateral materials, consultant fees, etc.)
   - Other

2. If you do not have a household budget, create one. Determine the monthly amount you need in order to cover the basic living expenses for you and your dependents without going into debt. Then determine if you need to either keep a current job or get a job with reliable and consistent income and benefits in order to meet those needs while you build your network marketing business.

3. Create a plan for paying off whatever debt you currently have. (Having an affordable mortgage on your home is the only exception to the no-debt rule.)

4. If you do not have enough liquefiable savings to support you and your dependents for at least six months, devise a savings plan. This monthly deposit into your savings account needs to be included in your household budget.

CHAPTER 2

What Is Your Intention?

Most people set goals in a vacuum with no connection to a greater purpose and to the people and priorities they care most about. When you set goals and make decisions within the context of what is truly important in your life, it's much easier to determine what matters and what doesn't.

As you set goals, do you ask yourself what you *want*, or do you ask yourself what you are *intending to attract*?

The word "want" typically represents things you wish to *have*. The word "intention" represents the experience you choose to create—how you wish to *be*. For example, you may *want* to eat some junk food, and that does not support your *intention* to *be* healthy.

Life is about choices. You make choices every single moment that move you toward or away from your intentions. Set goals and take action steps that are based on your *commitment to your intentions*, not on how you *feel* at any given moment. If you allow how you're feeling to determine whether or not you will take the action steps you've committed to, you probably won't follow through much of the time.

We've all heard the saying Perception Is Reality. Your perception of reality is what creates your reality. The key to changing your reality is to shift your focus. Here's an interesting exercise that exemplifies the power of focus:

Tell someone your life story or a life experience as if it were a tragedy, emphasizing all the terrible aspects of that experience.

Now tell the same story as an uplifting and delightful experience, focusing on all the good aspects of that same experience.

The actual facts do not change, but what you choose to focus on when you tell the story makes a huge difference in *how you feel* about your circumstances. As Wayne Dyer reminds us, *"If you change the way you look at things, the things you look at change."*

I coached a client (I'll call him Tom) who was a small business owner in the start-up phase of his business. He was working long hours, and he was stressed to the max. I had just taught Tom a weekly planning process that was designed to help him build greater balance into his life (see chapter 8). As Tom and I went through the planning process together, I asked him, "What are one or two intentions you have this week as a father?" He said, "I have to spend more time with my kids."

Since "have to" is victim language, I asked him, "Do you *have to* or do you *choose to* spend more time with your kids?" He was silent for a long time before he responded, "I *choose* to, and I have *never* thought of it that way before. I love my kids, and I want to spend more time with them. It's just that for so long, my wife has been nagging at me to leave the office and be more involved in my kids' lives that I never stopped to think about the fact that I really *do want* to spend more time with them!"

A week later, during our coaching appointment, Tom told me that he'd had one of the best weeks he could remember ever spending with his kids. He still had the same amount of work at the office. His circumstances had not changed, but he changed his *focus* from being the victim of a nagging wife and being a tyrant of a boss to himself to choosing a more active role as a father.

Language is very powerful. Quit "shoulding" on yourself and be at choice!

In addition to choosing empowering language that supports your intentions and desires, it's also important to use the power of visualization. One way to visualize what you choose is to describe your perfect average day. Once you have described it in detail, it will feel far more reachable and realistic than it ever has before—as if you have already experienced being, doing, or having it. As you create a vivid picture of what you desire and you stay focused on that vision, you will move toward it and start to create it.

One of the most amazing musical examples of the power of visualization is the story of how George Frederic Handel wrote his masterpiece, *Messiah*—including all the orchestration—in just twenty-four days. A servant's testimony reported that Handel locked himself in his study, often refusing food and surviving on minimal sleep. At the end of this three-week period, Handel burst out of his study with tears in his eyes and the *Messiah* script in his hand, declaring that he'd had a great vision and had seen "God in Heaven with a Company of Angels surrounding Him." This vision is what gave Handel the inspiration to write his masterpiece. He reportedly could not write fast enough as he transcribed what he heard in his head onto paper.

Having a vision can inspire you to do things you ordinarily would not do. I learned this when I first decided to write this book in 2007. My will to write it was not enough to turn intention into action. I did not yet have the vision or the clarity about why it was so important for me to write it. Once I was clear about my purpose and my intention for this book, the words flowed effortlessly from my brain onto the computer.

Frankly, it's hard to get what you want if you don't know what it is or why it's important. You can spend all your time complaining about what you *don't* want. But until you really know what you *do* want and why it's important to you, you will not take the necessary action to move toward it. If you don't know where you're going, any road will take you there.

Visualizing what you want—as if it already has happened—is incredibly powerful. The more vivid your vision, the more real it becomes.

Note: All the exercises in this book can be accessed through a website provided on page 155.

Desire is the starting point of all achievement, not a hope, not a wish, but a keen pulsating desire which transcends everything.

—Napoleon Hill

List 50 Things You Want to Do, Be, or Have

When you start, your list will probably include things like your dream home or dream car. As you go, it gets harder to list 50 things, and you may start listing silly things. Don't make judgments or edit as you write. Just keep writing whatever comes to mind, no matter how outrageous these things seem right now. Keep going until you have 50 things on your list. The core essence of what you want to do, be, or have will show up on your list when you start running out of the more superficial things.

To help you get started, first consider this question:**What intentions do you have?**

Write down what you'd like to *do, be, or have* in each of the categories listed below. Be aware of your self-talk. No "should, gotta, have to" language is allowed here. Begin each intention with "I choose to . . ."

- *Relationships:* family and friends

- *Health:* physical, mental, spiritual

- *Prosperity:* finances, lifestyle, time, possessions

- *Environment:* personal, local, global

- *Experiences:* what's on your "bucket list"

- *Contribution or legacy:* career, volunteer work, hobbies

Example: "I choose to . . ."

- *Relationships:* go out of town once a month with my spouse with a focus on our relationship

- *Health:* work with a personal trainer, hire a personal chef

- *Prosperity*: generate $_____ a year in interest from our investments

- *Environment:* professionally landscape the backyard, hire an interior decorator

- *Experiences:* go on a Hawaii cruise to four islands, go on a hot air balloon ride with friends

- *Contribution/legacy:* write my book, put the kids through college

As you've listed all the tangible things you could possibly ever imagine wanting, you may find yourself writing down some choices that contain deeper meaning or that represent leaving a legacy:

- Begin a foundation to help economically disadvantaged young adults start their own businesses.

- Experience joy in everything that I do regardless of external circumstances.

Identify three things that will absolutely be done, scheduled, or experienced within the next three months:

1

2

3

Even if you do not have the current resources to accomplish these things or you don't know how you will make it happen, you'll see opportunities emerge when you write these things down and schedule them in your calendar.

Your Perfect Average Day

Limitations live only in our minds. But if we use our imagination,
our possibilities become limitless.

—Jamie Paolinett, Cyclist

Close your eyes and let your subconscious play around with this question: *if there were no limitations or consequences, what would my perfect average day look like?*

Here are a few clarifications:

- "Average" means that you could do it every day and not die or get sick of it.

- "No limitations" means that your health, finances, geography, or other people do not limit you.

- "No consequences" means that you won't get into trouble for doing it.

Project yourself into the future and write down what a perfect average day looks like—using the present tense—as if you have already accomplished what you want to do, be, or have. If you have trouble getting started, use the five *W*s—who, what, when, where, why—as you describe your day. Describe it from the moment you awaken to the moment you fall asleep. Describe what you're doing, where you are, who you are with, and how you feel (the why behind it) throughout the day. Use as many senses as you can as you describe your perfect average day.

CHAPTER 3

Are You a Human *Being* or a Human *Doing?*

Success is not the key to happiness. Happiness is the key to success.
If you love what you are doing, you will be successful.

—*Albert Schweitzer*

Many people feel like they are running as fast as possible but are not getting where they want to go. Something very powerful rests at the core of all this—the lens through which we view our lives—also known as a *paradigm.*

Old paradigm: *do* so you can *have* so you can *be.*

New paradigm: *be* so you can *do* so you can *have.*

The old paradigm subscribes to the belief that what we *have* determines who we will *be.* One of my happiest and most fulfilled coaching clients was someone who had very little money and earthly possessions. One of the unhappiest clients I've ever worked with was a woman who had an abundance of money and material goods, yet her life was hollow and unfulfilling. She kept buying more things to fill a void.

How can one *have* everything they've ever wanted and yet *be* so empty and unhappy? And how can one *have* so little and yet *be* so happy and content? Happiness and fulfillment are not created by material wealth or possessions alone—what we *have*—but rather by who we are *being* and what we are *doing.*

I'm not suggesting that we all take a vow of poverty. There's nothing wrong with *having* things. The problems arise when we sacrifice who we are *being* for the sake of *having* more. When we do that, we will never *have* enough.

If you want to have more, you must become more.

—Jim Rohn

The new paradigm embraces the belief that when our life choices are informed by who we are *being* (our values and vision), what we *do* (our mission) is a natural extension of this, and what we *have (our possessions)* is enough.

When you operate under this new paradigm—*be* so you can *do* so you can *have*—you make a shift in your entire belief system. You are no longer willing to negotiate who you are *being* so you can *have* more.

Deepak Chopra reminds us that "everyone has a purpose in life . . . a unique gift or special talent to give to others. And when we blend this unique talent with service to others, we experience the ecstasy and exultation of our own spirit, which is the ultimate goal of all goals."

In 2007, I decided to write this book. I could not get beyond writing the outline. Again in 2008 I carved out time to write my book, and still nothing came. I was determined to *do* it. What I later discovered was that I had difficulty writing my book because the way I was *being* (overwhelmed and unbalanced) was not congruent with the core message of this book. Once my life focus shifted from *doing* more things to *being* in peace, balance, and harmony and aligning with my life purpose, the words started to naturally flow.

Looking back, I realize that 2007-2008 were heavy personal development years for me, and I was stirring up a lot of my own beliefs. I was in the midst of making a huge paradigm shift. By November 2010, I felt compelled to write this book, and I could not stop it! I sat down at the keyboard and effortlessly downloaded the words from my brain onto my computer. I finished writing the first draft on 1/1/11—just two months later.

The power of making this shift applies to everyone, whether you are writing a book or building a network marketing business. Who are you *being* right now?

 KATHY PAAUW

If you are not currently living the life of your dreams, which of these five reasons do you most relate to?

1. **You don't really know what you want, so you just "get by" each day, doing whatever is necessary to pay the bills or get through each day.** If you are living for your time off (evenings, weekends, holidays), this may be you. People who do what they love look forward to going to work as well as having free time.

2. **You are operating under someone else's definition of success, which does not match yours.** Most often, this is a result of something that was passed down from a parent or another close relative whom you don't want to disappoint.

3. **You know what you want, but limiting beliefs hold you back or create obstacles to your success.** You may have opted for a career track because you did not believe you could support yourself doing what you truly love. Perhaps you've told yourself that you aren't good enough or capable enough to do something you really want to do.

4. **You know what you want, but you don't know how to get it. You aren't sure what steps to take, so you do nothing.** Instead of asking *how*, ask *what*. "What is one thing I can do today that will help me move in the direction I want to go?"

   Focusing on the "how" stops most people dead in their tracks because their response is usually "I don't know." The "what" may be as simple as doing some Internet research or having a conversation with someone who can offer good advice about next steps to take to move you toward reaching your goal.

   If you have not yet started your own network marketing business because you are not sure which company is the best fit for you, I highly recommend reading *License to Dream: Every Woman's Guide to Financial Freedom through Network Marketing* by Judy O'Higgins, Kristi Lee, and Karen Palmer. Although this book was written especially for women, it offers tips that will help anyone with the selection process. This book also offers solid tips on how to get started.

5. **You know the action steps to take to move you toward reaching your goals, but you don't have enough time to fit one more thing into your busy life**. The issue here is not really a matter of time but of discipline and priorities. "Not enough time" is a very common excuse for staying stuck. Ask yourself what you can say no to that is a lower priority for you. For example, the average person in Western culture spends four hours a day watching television. What would happen if you devoted just one of those hours each day toward reaching an important goal? That's seven hours a week that you can repurpose!

I have been inspired by a couple who recently built a strong network marketing business in our company in record time. In less than five months—and with no previous network marketing experience—this husband-and-wife team did what it has taken most people several years to do. They got promoted three times. They did all this despite the demands of his thriving medical practice and raising three active young children—including coaching several soccer teams! When I hear people say that they are "too busy" to build their business, I think of this physician and his wife. How have they been able to build their tremendously successful business on the side in such a short time? They are highly motivated, and nothing will stop them from achieving their dream of enjoying lifestyle freedom and helping others do the same. He recently said to me, "The emotional and spiritual wealth that network marketing has brought to my life is something I never expected. I am more at peace today than I ever have been. To wake up smiling each day is a feeling everyone should experience."

Once you've identified the primary obstacle above, there's another key ingredient to your success. Your environments play a huge role in your success and failure. The second section of this book will address the role of environments in your life.

 KATHY PAAUW

FREEDOM CHALLENGE

Work/Life Balance Assessment

Please place a *T* (true) or *F* (false) next to each of the following statements:

1. I feel stressed out most of the time.

2. My family/friends frequently complain that I don't spend enough time with them.

3. I seldom take time off from work to enjoy non work-related things I love to do.

4. I keep working harder, but my income does not reflect the number of hours I'm putting in.

5. I have not had a vacation in the last two years.

6. In addition to working all day, I frequently work into the evenings and on weekends.

7. I feel exhausted most of the time.

8. My sleep is often disrupted by worries or thoughts I cannot turn off.

9. I do not carve out time to exercise on a regular basis.

10. I often work while I am eating.

The more *true* statements you've identified, the more you are living with the old paradigm and the faster you are moving toward burnout.

In chapter 7, you will be introduced to a time management matrix. The exercises at the end of that chapter will help you make the shift to the new paradigm: *be* so you can *do* so you can *have*.

Before you can move forward, it's helpful to be clear about what is stopping you. If you are not currently living the life of your dreams, which of these five reasons do you most relate to?

1. You don't really know what you want, so you just "get by" each day, doing whatever is necessary to pay the bills.

2. You are operating under someone else's definition of success, which does not match yours.

3. You know what you want, but limiting beliefs hold you back or create obstacles to your success.

4. You know what you want, but you don't know how to get it. You aren't sure what steps to take, so you do nothing.

5. You know the action steps to take to move you toward reaching your goals, but you don't have enough time to fit one more thing into your busy life.

Define Freedom

The word "freedom" means many things to different people. If you could do what you want to do, when you want to do it, with whom you want to do it, and where and how you want to do it, what would that look like in your life? What are the indicators or signs you would look for that would confirm that you are experiencing freedom as you define it?

CHAPTER 4

Affirmations— Lyrics to the Music of your Heart

Your visions will become clear only when you look into your heart.
Who looks outside, dreams. Who looks inside, awakens.

—Carl Jung

You were created with a genius that is unique to you. When you tap into your true essence—the music of your heart—amazing things will begin to happen in your life.

If you are familiar with the law of attraction—you attract more of whatever you focus on—you may already be familiar with the power of affirmations. An affirmation is a statement that you send to yourself on a daily basis to condition your subconscious mind. Each affirmation begins with the words "I am . . ."

Short, simple, and precise "I am" statements are the most powerful. Keep it in the present tense and keep it positive. In other words, your affirmations focus on what you intend to attract into your life rather than what you don't want.

Here are two versions of an affirmation statement:

1. I am debt free.

2. I am financially independent and free.

The first statement puts the focus on debt—what you don't want. The second statement focuses on the desired outcome—freedom.

Whenever possible, include a feeling word. Here are two more examples:

1. We are living in our dream home.

2. We are joyfully building lasting memories as a family in our dream home on the lake.

The second statement elicits more feelings than the first one. Great vision statements evoke emotion and excitement.

I learned the incredible power of an "I am" statement when I created a negative one without realizing it. During the first quarter of 2007, I lived with a constant feeling of being overwhelmed. The more I thought about feeling overwhelmed, the stronger the feeling got. In March of that year, I had a conversation with a friend I had not seen in years. She had heard me sing the national anthem at a Seattle Mariner's game years before. Remembering that I was a singer, she told me that I needed to audition for a local theater company's production of *The Sound of Music*—my all-time favorite musical. My reply, "There's no possible way I could fit *one* more thing into my hectic schedule. I am overwhelmed as it is!" She stopped me mid-rant and said, "*What* did you just say?" I said, "I am overwhelmed!"

When I heard myself say it a second time, I realized that this had been a powerful "I am" statement I'd been repeating for several months. No wonder I was feeling like such a crazy person! That was the "nourishment" I had fed my brain. I realized it was time to write a new "I am" statement to replace the one that was keeping me stuck feeling overwhelmed.

> *Those who program themselves for success find a way to succeed even in the most difficult of circumstances. Solutions to most problems come from one source and one source alone: yourself.*
>
> —*Napoleon Hill*

Here's the new statement I created: *"I have all the time I need for what's most important to me."*

When I catch myself beginning to feel overwhelmed, this "I am" statement helps me remember the truth. I really do have all the time I need for what's most important to me. My job is to sort the priorities! What a difference this shift has made in my life.

I decided to audition for *The Sound of Music*, and I was cast as one of the nuns. I was the solo voice that opened the show each night. I had a blast performing that summer in my favorite musical! I had not performed in a stage production for twenty-two years, and I had so much fun being part of a cast again.

You will get what you consistently focus on even if you focus on *not* getting something. For example, *don't think about a pink elephant with polka dots.* (As you read that, I'll bet you were imagining a pink elephant with polka dots!) Most people focus on what they don't want and wonder why they keep getting more of it!

Here's an interesting sequence of how things work:

> Words produce thoughts.
> Thoughts produce feelings.
> Feelings produce decisions.
> Decisions produce actions.
> Actions produce habits.
> Habits create character.
> Character determines your destiny.

If you want to change the direction of your life in some way, it all begins with the word choices you feed to your brain. That's why your affirmation statements are so powerful. It's also important that you have a filter in place to limit the amount of "negative" you see and hear through the media and the people you encounter on a daily basis.

Your brain is like a heat-seeking missile. It will lock in on goals you've clearly identified. Scientists have determined that the brain uses its own reticular activating system to filter through the millions of images, sounds, impressions, and other messages we receive each day and to let into our conscious mind only that information we need to survive or to meet specific goals we have identified. When you decide what you want, you instruct the brain to start looking for information, resources, opportunities, and other ways to achieve them.

In Tony Rubleski's book *Mind Capture: How to Awaken Your Entrepreneurial Genius in a Time of Great Economic Change*, he emphasizes the importance of reprogramming the mind for achievement. He points out that many network marketing professionals encounter six typical challenges:

1. Lots of rejection

2. Confusion and criticism from those who are often closest to them

3. Negative perceptions that are often untrue about the industry or company they've joined

4. A big shift in mind-set to becoming proactive and entrepreneurial

5. Creation of new habits and better time management skills to achieve advancement

6. The old get-rich-quick mentality most people still have in their minds

The biggest enemy to most businesses is fear and rejection. Gaining mastery over these is essential to your success in network marketing. As a singer, I know something about these emotions, which are close cousins to each other.

I've sung the national anthem in a ballpark packed with fifty-one thousand baseball fans attending a national league division play-off game. I've also sung for a group of twenty-five people in someone's living room. Which performance do you think I felt the most nervous for? You may be surprised—it was the living room performance. Why? Because standing on the field at the ballpark, I could not see any individual faces—just a mass of people. The living room was a much more intimate audience to sing for, and I felt more vulnerable because I could see each person's facial expressions if they rejected me. Of course, I could also see their expressions if they loved me.

Where does this fear come from? It originates between your ears in the form of self-talk. The more you want something, the more you have to lose if you don't get it and the easier it is to allow fear to take over. To overcome fear, you must tap into the emotion that accompanies what you *do* want instead of focusing on the emotion

   KATHY PAAUW

that accompanies what you are afraid of. You must also let go of your attachment to the outcome. One of the best ways to do this is to learn how to love people for who they are. You love them whether they decided to work with you or not.

The individuals who succeed in this profession are the ones who have the fortitude to withstand the trying times and keep the focus on what is right and what they have rather than on what is wrong and what they don't have. All network marketing companies go through challenges. Successful network marketing professionals learn to look forward, not back. Your affirmation statements will keep you focused on the future that you choose.

One note of caution about your affirmations is this: create statements that help you visualize a growing and thriving team without having any attachment to the outcome of *how* it will grow. When you get attached to the *how* (who will join your team, who your builders will be, etc.), you will often be disappointed.

In any deck of cards, you get four aces in the deck. Your job is to sort through your list of prospects, looking for the aces, not expending energy trying to turn a prospect into an ace of hearts when they are really a six of spades. All the wishing in the world will not change the face of the card! The same holds true with prospects. Share your business opportunity without attachment to the outcome and allow people who are attracted to what you have to offer to join you. We will talk more about letting go of the attachment to the outcome in chapter 12.

Once you gain clarity about your intentions, it's vital that you identify the compelling *why* that will provide the fuel to propel you toward accomplishing your goals. Hook into as many of your five senses (sight, hearing, touch, taste, smell) as you can when creating your *why* statement. The more senses you use, the more emotions and feelings you will tap into, which will help you overcome the effects of fear.

If you've spent much time with a preschool-age child, you know that they ask a lot of *why* questions. As soon as you answer one question, they ask why again! I remember twenty years ago when our daughter, Carly, was asking *why* questions about a drunk guy sleeping on a sidewalk in the middle of Seattle's Pike Place Market on a very busy Saturday afternoon. People were actually stepping over him, and that got her attention. Here's how the conversation went:

Carly: Why is that man sleeping?
Me: Because he doesn't feel good.
Carly: Why doesn't he feel good?
Me: Because he drank too much alcohol.
Carly: Why did he drink too much alcohol?
Me: Because he's an alcoholic.
Carly: Why is he an alcoholic?
Me: Because he has a disease that makes him want to drink too much alcohol.
Carly: Why does he want to drink too much alcohol?

At this point, I changed the subject! I was not prepared to explain alcoholism to a four-year-old.

This is actually a great technique to use to get to the "why behind the why." The process is like peeling an onion because we often protect the core essence of our *why* with more superficial responses. Keep asking *why* until you've reached the core. Another way of asking the question is to say, "So what?" and then answer, "So that I can ___."

I'll provide an example by sharing my life purpose statement, which is also one of my "I am" statements. Because one's core purpose generally does not change over time, my statement is the same today as it was when I wrote it fourteen years ago.

Affirmation: I am a divine messenger of peace, compassionately infusing balance and harmony.

Why (so what)? So that I can help others live a balanced and healthy life while enjoying the journey along the way.

Why (so what)? So that each of us as individuals can experience living in harmony and peace.

Why (so what)? So that we can ultimately experience world peace.

When you keep peeling the onion until you get to the core, you'll identify the compelling *why* that provides the motivation necessary to propel you forward in reaching your goals.

When I feel like giving up, a review of my purpose statement—my *why*—motivates me to keep going. My statement reminds me that all of God's creation is divine—including me—which reminds me of the responsibility that I have to be a good steward of the gifts I have been given. My statement also reminds me of my core values—peace, balance, and harmony.

Let me illustrate my point about the power of your *why* with a hypothetical example:

> You have been earning an average of $3,000 a month in your network marketing business. Next month you've set a goal to earn $9,000—a huge stretch for you. What are the chances that you will reach your goal?
>
> Let's add more information to this scenario. Your child was just diagnosed with a serious illness. There is a cure, and the cost for the treatment is $9,000. Without receiving this treatment in the next month, your beloved child will die. You have no health insurance, no savings, no credit, and no personal family or friends who can help you pay for it. You've got to come up with the money yourself.

Has your *why* for reaching your goal just become more compelling? Is there *anything* that would stop you from earning or raising the $9,000 needed if it meant the difference between life and death for your own child? You must recruit your heart and soul to help you with such a goal as that will provide the passion you'll need to fuel your entrepreneurial engine when times get tough.

Your *why* for building your network marketing business may not be as dramatic as the example above. I share this example to convey the power of heart, soul, and passion. This is what will carry you through the challenging times. You are unwilling to "settle," and you have an unshakable drive to move ahead even in the midst of extreme challenges.

Once you have created your affirmation statements and have identified the *compelling why* behind them, it's time to identify some persistent actions to make it happen! We call this attr*ACTION!*

Affirmation without discipline is the beginning of delusion.
—Jim Rohn

KATHY PAAUW

FREEDOM CHALLENGE

*Cherish your visions and your dreams, as they are the children
of your soul, the blueprints of your ultimate achievements.*

—Napoleon Hill

What you feed your mind is what you will send out to the world. What you send out comes back. What are the affirmation statements that you choose to feed your mind on a daily basis? Write your statements beginning with "I am . . ." Write it as if you are already being, doing, or having what you choose. Then write the *why* behind each statement. Write the *why* as many times as you need to in order to arrive at the core. It may help begin your answer to *why* with "So that I can ___"

I am ____

    Why? ____

    Why? ____

I am ____

    Why? ____

    Why? ____

I am ____

    Why? ____

    Why? ____

I am ____

    Why? ____

    Why? ____

Create a vision board and look at it every day. Pictures connect with your emotions. When you see a picture that depicts exactly what you want, your vision will become even more crystal clear. This will accelerate your progress toward reaching your goals. Get some poster board, glue sticks, scissors, and lots of magazines and have a vision board party with your team and create your vision boards together.

You may also create a digital corkboard using the Ultimate Vision Board for images of your goals. Visit *www.facebook.com/visionboard* for a free tool that will help you with this. You can even e-mail this digital vision board to friends and colleagues.

PART TWO

Create Your Path to Freedom

CHAPTER 5

The Nine Environments of You

In 2007 and 2008, I spent a significant amount of time doing some personal development work with three amazing coaches. I will be forever grateful to Jack Canfield (best-selling author of many books, including *The Success Principles*), Jim Bunch (creator of *The Ultimate Game of Life* coaching program), and Hale Dwoskin (author of *The Sedona Method*).

One of the coaching models I was introduced to by Jim Bunch is called *The Nine Environments of You*. This model was originally created by the late Thomas Leonard—considered by many to be the founder of the coaching profession—whom Jim worked with privately up until the time of Leonard's death in 2003.

The nine environments model provides an outstanding tool that enables you to identify where your life may be out of balance or where your level of satisfaction is low. Once you are aware of this, you can "upgrade" your environments in a way that will support the ultimate lifestyle freedom you desire. This is done by choosing action steps you will take to increase your level of satisfaction in each of these areas of your life.

The environments you maintain in and around you will create wealth from within, which ultimately allows the external wealth to flow into your life. Most people are in pursuit of external wealth without having an awareness of the collective power that all our environments hold. When all your environments are in balance, you'll experience synchronicity. Remarkable "coincidences" will happen in your life as things fall into place. The end result is that you will attract what you desire with much greater ease.

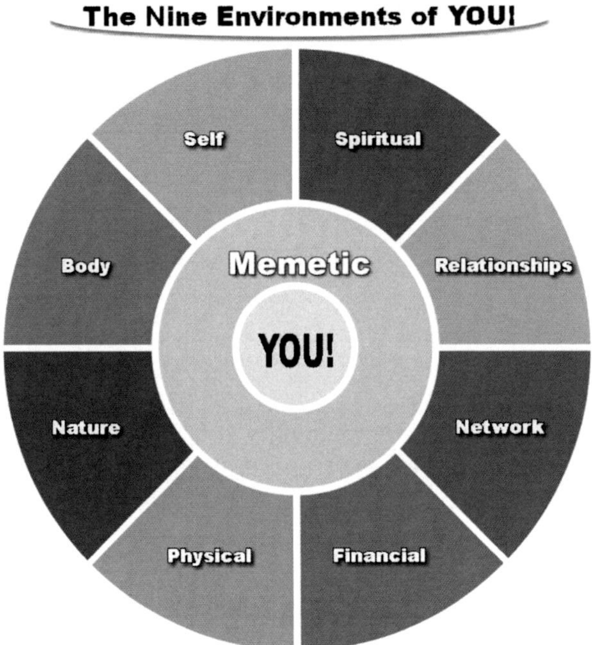

This model is shared with permission from CoachVille LLC, *www.coachville.com*, 1-973-601-9444

An Overview of Thomas Leonard's Nine Environments of You

- *Memetic:* the lens through which you view the world, including the other eight environments—beliefs, values, ideas, thoughts, cultural norms, frameworks
- *Body:* physical appearance, health, energy
- *Self:* personality, temperament, character, gifts, talents, strengths
- *Spiritual:* deep connections (may or may not be religious in nature)
- *Relationships:* family, close friends and colleagues, support personnel
- *Network:* greater community, strategic partners, customers, professional connections, social networks
- *Financial:* money (income, expenses), investments, budgeting
- *Physical:* places (home, office, car—wherever you spend time), sounds, lighting, furnishings, tangible objects
- *Nature:* outdoors, beauty, seasons, cycle of life

KATHY PAAUW

If you've ever gone from working in a cluttered and disorganized office to experiencing the calm and peace of clearing out the clutter, you've experienced an environmental design change. Or maybe you've tried to get some work done in a stuffy public place where there was an argument going on nearby, and you moved outside to get away from the exchange of harsh words and to enjoy fresh air, peace, and quiet. You've experienced another environmental design change.

Can you relate to these examples? If so, you know the power that your environments have over you and how important it is that you design these environments so they support you. Our environments work in harmony with each other.

Just as many environmental elements work together to support your goals, many musical elements work together to create a song: melody, rhythm, rests, note value, harmony, tempo, dynamics, etc. When some of these elements are missing or are not in alignment with each other, a song sounds "off." Imagine listening to a song that was written with no rests or one written with all notes having the same pitch or note value.

Well-designed environments are the key to your success in anything you want to achieve. In this section of the book, my goal is to help you design winning environments that support and inspire you. I'll tell some stories and share examples of how you can "upgrade" each of your nine environments. My Freedom Challenges at the end of this section will help you apply this model to your life.

1. **Memetic Environment**: the lens through which you view the world: beliefs, values, ideas, thoughts, cultural norms, frameworks

   Whatever the mind can conceive and believe, it can achieve.

   —W. Clement Stone

The word "memetic" comes from the Latin word "meme." According to Wikipedia, "a meme is a unit of social information. It is a relatively newly coined term and identifies ideas or beliefs that are transmitted from one person or group of people to another."

The world is full of ideas and beliefs that have been passed down from one generation to the next. Whatever you focus on expands. The question is, what ideas or beliefs does your mind focus on? How does this impact your ability to manifest your intentions for your life?

As you identify what makes your heart sing, you will discover motifs. A motif is a short melodic idea. These small pieces of melody will appear again and again in a piece of music, sometimes exactly the same and sometimes changed. When a motif returns, it can be slower or faster, in a different key, or with the pitches or rhythms altered. The first movement of Beethoven's Symphony No. 5 has the most famous motif in Western classical music, known as the fate motif.

A motif can be an affirmation or a limiting belief. What are you repeating over and over? So often, people focus on what they do not have or have not yet achieved. This becomes a "motif" in their life. The more you focus on what has not yet occurred, the more your attention—your point of attraction—is on the fact that you do *not* have what you want. Since we get more of whatever we focus on, we continue to get more of what we don't want. Change the motif to an affirmation—act as if you already have what you want and focus on that—and it will more easily manifest in your life.

Notice that the Memetic environment touches all other eight environments in the model. That's because everything gets filtered through your mind. As you grow up, various people in your life—aunts, uncles, parents, grandparents, friends, teachers, and the cultural norms you learn from society—send you messages that "program" your mind. This forms your thoughts and beliefs about yourself, others, and the world you live in.

If you want to change anything in any of your environments, it begins with the thoughts that you think and the language you use with yourself and others.

KATHY PAAUW

I grew up in a family that had enough money to live very comfortably. When I was a child, my parents would say, "When you go to college . . .," so there was always the assumption that my siblings and I would go to college. Because there was plenty of money and my parents told us they would support us through college, none of us established college savings accounts. Whatever money I earned in high school was spent on clothes, makeup, contributions to a child I sponsored in the Philippines, donations to my church, and entertainment.

Just before entering my senior year of high school, I learned that my parents had not saved any money for our college educations and they were filing for bankruptcy. I also learned that they were getting a divorce. By the time I was eighteen, I was on my own. Because I had been declared as a dependent on my parents' tax returns the year before, their income disqualified me from receiving any financial aid.

I decided that I was going to college no matter what, and I got busy figuring out how to make it happen. My first year in college, I took out regular bank loans because I did not qualify for need-based scholarship assistance, student loans, or even work-study programs on campus. Although it was a challenge, I supported myself through four years of study at a private college and got my bachelor's degree.

In Jack Canfield's book *The Success Principles*, this is Principle #1: take 100 percent responsibility for your life. Although Jack's book had not yet been written, I believe that it was this fundamental principle that supported me in deciding to attend college.

Jack shares a powerful equation:

$$E + R = O$$

Event + Response = Outcome

In order to change the sum (what comes after the equal sign), you must change a variable. We often cannot change the *events* that take place in our lives, but we *can* change our *response* to those events. By doing so, we can change the *outcome.*

Here is an example of how the response one chooses affects the outcome:

Event: My parents filed for bankruptcy and got a divorce.
Response #1: I can't go to college because Mom and Dad can't pay for it (victim response).
Outcome: No college education

Event: My parents filed for bankruptcy and got a divorce.
Response #2: I'm going to college, no matter what it takes (100 percent responsibility).
Outcome: Earned a college degree

> *Ninety-nine percent of all failures come from*
> *people who have a habit of making excuses.*
>
> —*George Washington Carver*

As my good friend, Kody Bateman, always says, "The stories of your mind become the stories of your life." Kody is the author of *Promptings: Your Inner Guide to Making a Difference.* This book provides an outstanding blueprint for how to clean up your Memetic environment and install the beliefs that will enable you to move your life forward in powerful and meaningful ways.

Memetic Environment Upgrade Example

Upgrades desired

- Rework my self-talk by replacing "I can't . . ." with "I am . . ."
- Clarify and enforce my boundaries with others.
- Remember that I cannot be all things to all people.

Actions to be taken by when

- Install new beliefs by reading my "I am" statements every morning while coffee is brewing.
- Leave the room or end a conversation as soon as someone becomes disrespectful.

- Say no to things that are not priorities for me. Wait for twenty-four hours before responding to requests of my time that fall outside the bounds of my current responsibilities.

2. **Body Environment:** physical appearance, health, energy

You may not have previously thought of the body as an environment, but it is. You are *not* your body; your body is something you have, and it can be designed. The Body environment includes clothing, hair, mass, and energy.

In music, the body is represented by the physical paper that a composition is printed on or the CD that a recording is burned onto. Without printed music, it would be difficult for musicians to learn their parts for a new song. Without CDs or sound files, it would be difficult for musical compositions to be shared around the world.

Is your own body a source of inspiration to you? Is it strong, flexible, and healthy? A positive body image is one of the most important aspects of happiness and well-being, yet it is an area which often seems to be a challenge for many. Creating strength, energy, and well-being through daily practices is an essential part of winning in the game of life.

When you got your first car, you were probably aware that you could replace it later. If someone had told you that this was the only car you'd ever have, you would most likely have taken better care of it than you did. Unlike a car, we only get one body. We cannot expect to abuse a car—or our bodies—and enjoy a long and productive life.

Oprah's personal trainer, Bob Greene, has teamed up with psychologist Ann Kearney-Cooke to write a book called *The Life You Want: Get Motivated, Lose Weight and Be Happy.* What Greene has discovered over the years is that only 20 percent of people who lose weight keep it off. That's because they don't deal with the emotional issues that caused the weight gain in the first place. Greene's book helps people identify significant motivating factors, which he calls "emotional incentives" for staying active and eating healthy. A study found that when one's focus is on *happiness*, unwanted weight comes off and stays off. When one's focus is on *weight loss*, the results are short-term.

Dr. Dean Ornish, a clinical professor of medicine at University of California San Francisco and author of the book *Love and Survival,* tells us that medicine today focuses primarily on drugs, surgery, genes, and germs. Yet love and intimacy are at the root of what makes us sick and what makes us well. Connections with other people affect not only the quality of our lives but also our survival. Numerous studies have concluded that people who feel lonely are many times more likely to get heart disease than those who have a strong sense of connection and community. People are four times more likely to have a heart attack within six months of losing someone close to them through death or divorce.

This year marked the 30th anniversary of my father's death. When people ask how he died at such an early age—he was forty-seven—I tell them that he died of a broken heart. I attribute much of my father's heart disease to the high stress he was under as well an unwillingness to honor his own needs for a healthier diet and regular exercise. There was one more contributing factor to his fatal heart attack: my parents had just divorced, and my father was very lonely.

It's ironic that my father died from a heart attack on Valentine's Day—a day that we plaster hearts all over everything as a way to recognize those we love. The night before he died, his office assistant was visiting him in the hospital intensive care unit. He asked her to write down a message and put it in a valentine for his children. Because he was so heavily sedated, she told him that she would come back in the morning to take down his words. He begged her, "*Please* . . . take my message *now* . . . I'm going to *die.*" She dismissed his request—chastising him for talking such silly nonsense about dying—and said she would be back in the morning.

Even in his heavily medicated state, my father wanted to reach out and feel connected. He wanted me and my siblings to know that he loved us. His parting gift to us was a handwritten message I will always treasure. Sometime before 2:00 a.m. on Valentine's Day, my father expressed his final wishes that each of us experience love, joy, and peace. Dad's homemade valentine—scrawled on the back of a used envelope—was found at his hospital bedside after he was pronounced dead.

The studies cited in Greene's and Ornish's books provide additional proof that our nine environments are so interconnected. Happiness (Self environment) and feeling connected (Relationships, Network, and Spiritual environments) have the amazing power to reduce heart disease and help people maintain weight loss (Body environment).

KATHY PAAUW

Do you treat your body as if you could just swap out parts when you need them, or do you treat it with the utmost care that it deserves? How are you managing the other environments in your life that enhance or impair your physical health and fitness?

Body Environment Upgrade Example

Upgrades desired

- Feel rested when I wake up.
- Get fit, toned, and healthy.
- Reduce stress and increase a sense of peace in my life.

Actions to be taken by when

- Go to bed by (time) each night.
- Ask (name) to commit to daily thirty-minute walks at least five times a week. If weather is bad, commit to walking in a mall or other indoor facility.
- Meditate fifteen minutes a day beginning (date). Research which recorded meditation program I will use and select one by (date).

3. **Self Environment:** personality, temperament, character, gifts, talents, strengths

Self is another environment that is often forgotten. Each of us was born with a unique personality, temperament, gifts, talents, and strengths.

In musical terms, this is reflected by the theme, character, or mood of a song. Think about the effect music has on your emotions while you are watching a movie. Eliminating the musical sound track from a scary movie would vastly reduce the intensity of your experience while watching the thriller scenes. Imagine watching the movie *Jaws* without the haunting music that built up the suspense and fear before each shark attack.

Many people never fully express their personality or utilize the natural gifts and strengths they were given. Realized or not, you possess talents that you were born with. These talents may feel so natural that you don't even realize how they make you unique and special. Your combined unique talents and capabilities create an experience for others that cannot be exactly duplicated by anyone else because there is only one unique *you* in this world.

Years ago, I participated in a workshop series called *Authentic Promotion* taught by my friend and colleague, Master Certified Coach Molly Gordon. A few weeks into the workshop series, Molly mentioned something about stewardship. When I hear that word, I always think of church in the fall when a layperson asks the members to pledge support to the church for the coming year. Usually they say something like this: "All that we have has been given to us. It is our responsibility to give back a portion of what we have been given." As Molly was talking about stewardship in the context of marketing, I realized that I had always misunderstood what marketing was all about.

As soon as I stopped thinking about "selling" my services and started thinking about being a good steward of the gifts and talents I had been given, I completely shifted the way I felt about marketing. I was simply offering the gifts that I had been given—my coaching services—with no attachment to the other person's decision. Once I made my shift from *selling* to *authentic promotion* of what I had to offer, my coaching business doubled over the next twelve months.

As a good steward of whatever you've been given, it's not just a *good idea* for you to share your gifts and talents with others—it's your *responsibility* to do so. When you withhold what you have been given, you deprive others of receiving something they may need. I feel the same way about what I have to offer as a network marketing professional. It would be selfish for me to withhold a product or service that I thought could benefit someone else. If the other person chooses not to receive what I have to offer, I have no attachment to their decision. I have responsibly shared it, and I simply move on.

Marcus Buckingham and Donald Clifton, authors of *Now, Discover Your Strengths*, define talents as "*any recurring pattern of thought, feeling or behavior that can be productively applied.*" Here are some examples of talent as they define it: inquisitive, charming, persistent, responsible, and dyslexic. All these qualities can be productively applied.

Dyslexic? How could one consider dyslexia a talent?

     KATHY PAAUW

The authors shared an example of how David Boies—a celebrated trial attorney and one of the best litigators in the United States—frequently uses dyslexia to his advantage. He was recruited as counsel for the US government's antitrust suit against Microsoft in part because of his gift of dyslexia. Why? His dyslexia causes him to avoid using long and complicated words. He knows what these words mean but doesn't use them in his arguments because he's afraid that he will mispronounce them. This need to rely on simple words makes his arguments easy to follow. As a result, he comes across as a commonsense "man of the people," which naturally helps him win over a judge and jury.

The authors point out that *for David Boies, dyslexia is a talent because he has figured out a way to apply this recurring pattern productively, and by combining it with knowledge and skills, to turn it into a strength.*

Research has found that only 41 percent of Americans believe that the key to success is to focus on strengths rather than weaknesses. In Japan and China, only 24 percent of those surveyed said they'd focus on strengths. The rest of the population believed that the key to success is found by focusing on weaknesses and trying to improve them.

The problem is that we tend to get more of what we focus on. If we focus on our weaknesses, what does that mean?

The clearer you are about your own natural talents, the more you can focus on employing them in your everyday life. Whatever you set your mind to, you will be most successful and feel most fulfilled when you design your life to utilize your most dominant talents.

One great benefit of being part of a team in network marketing is that we can play to our strengths and talents and we can call on others to fill in with their strengths and talents in our weaker areas. One way to strengthen a team is to sponsor your weaknesses. What do I mean by that? Here's an example. If you have trouble meeting new people, sponsor someone who loves to meet people. If your public speaking skills are weak, sponsor someone who has great public speaking skills.

I love to teach and write, and I attract some of my prospects by offering free newsletters and workshops. I know someone else in our company who loves going to lots of formal networking events. We are both successful at building our teams because we focus on duplicable activities that we love and that we are good at doing.

Are you fully expressing your authentic self as you were created to?

Self Environment Upgrade Example

Upgrades desired

- Get back into singing regularly
- Decide if I will do public speaking.

Actions to be taken by when

- Join choir at church beginning next month.
- Visit a Toastmasters group in my area by (date).
- Decide if I want to begin offering teleclasses by (date).

4. **Spiritual Environment:** deep connections (may or may not be religious in nature)

Are you getting your energy from negative points of power such as apathy, grief, fear, lust, control, overwhelm, clutter, addictions, manipulation, and anger, or from positive points of power such as love, truth, courageousness, beauty, gratitude, and peace? As with all design choices, you can choose to get energy from the highest of sources, which ultimately come from living in a way that honors your soul.

I have a spiritual practice of letting go of my attachment to the outcome (see chapter 12). A wise friend reminded me that there are only three kinds of challenges:

- My own challenges
- Someone else's challenges
- God's challenges (challenges beyond human capability to solve)

Thinking of life's challenges in this way makes it easier for me to decide what to do next. Sometimes a challenge is bigger than I can manage. I give these to God and ask for guidance, wisdom, patience, and peace as I work through it. Letting go is a very powerful part of my spiritual practice.

I love the *Story of Two Wolves*. As the story goes, an elderly Cherokee Native American was teaching his grandchildren about life. He said to them, "A fight is going on inside me. It is a terrible fight and it is between two wolves. One wolf is evil—he is fear, anger, envy, sorrow, regret, greed, arrogance, self-pity, guilt, resentment, inferiority, lies, false pride, competition, superiority, and ego. The other is good—he is joy, peace, love, hope, sharing, serenity, humility, kindness, benevolence, friendship, empathy, generosity, truth, compassion, and faith. This same fight is going on inside you, and inside every other person too." They thought about it for a minute, and then one child asked his grandfather, "Which wolf will win, Grandfather?" The elder simply replied, "The one you feed."

A great way to get positive energy is to have a plan for ways to nourish your mind and soul. When you consider what most people feed their brains, it's usually pretty negative stuff. I encourage you to design a personal development plan that incorporates several senses—*reading, hearing* (CDs and downloads), *seeing* (visualization), *experiencing* (attending workshops and events), and *teaching* others what you have learned. Set a goal to read or listen to at least one personal development book a month.

Music can help you feel a spiritual connection because a song can hook deeply into your emotions. In addition, music often contains lyrics with powerful messages that feed your mind and soul. You may have learned lyrics to a song many years ago, and you can still remember the words. I learned the words to the song *Fifty Nifty United States* in grade school. To this day, I can still recite the fifty states in alphabetical order in less than one minute. If these same words had not been set to melody, I highly doubt I could still remember them. Words set to music have a way of sticking with us.

I have recorded a song that conveys the core message of this book, and you can listen to it or download it at *www.TheMusicOfYourHeart.com/song*. You'll find the lyrics to my song near the back of this book.

Be selective about what you expose yourself to. Do the lyrics of the songs you regularly listen to contain positive messages? Does the music uplift you? Are you selective about how much news you read, watch, or hear? Most of what we see on television, hear on the radio, or read in the newspaper is negative, so it's important to limit your exposure.

One of the greatest benefits of having a network marketing business is the personal development that is required in order to be successful. All healthy network marketing companies have a built-in personal development program as part of their company offerings. These personal development programs develop future leaders in our companies.

> *Each of us has a winner and a loser inside of us. The winner is up for the risk, but the loser thinks only of safety and security. Every time we let our fears, our doubts, or our low self-esteem win, the loser emerges and holds sway. Learning to share your vision and tell a powerful, persuasive story is learning how to override the loser inside you and allowing the winner to rise to the surface. Network marketing gives you the opportunity to face your fears, deal with them, overcome them, and bring out the winner that you have living inside you.*
>
> —*Robert Kiyosaki, The Business of the 21ˢᵗ Century*

Networking Times is a great bimonthly publication that I recommend for all network marketing professionals. There are also many wonderful books written for our profession. I recommend a couple, in particular, written by two highly respected and successful network marketing professionals of our time: (1) *Beach Money*, by Jordan Adler, offers inspiring stories that teach powerful lessons that will help you create residual income; (2) *Making the First Circle Work*, by Randy Gage, teaches you how to take responsibility for your own success. The first circle is you!

My most powerful spiritual practice is to begin each day by expressing gratitude. Gratitude opens the heart so that life-expanding thoughts and ideas can easily enter your consciousness. Regardless of your present life circumstances, there's always something to be grateful for. What you focus on expands. When you focus on your inner voice, there are no limitations. Those limitations only exist through the outer voices and opinions of others, which are typically based on scarcity and limiting beliefs.

Spiritual Environment Upgrade Example:

Upgrade desired

- Enjoy a sense of peace, regardless of my circumstances or experiences.

Actions to be taken by when

- Pray daily, give my worries to God, and let go.
- Include at least one thing I appreciated about today in my daily e-mail report to my accountability partner.

5. **Relationships Environment:** family, close friends and colleagues, support personnel

You are the average of the five people you spend the most time with.

—Jim Rohn

If you want to know someone really well, simply get to know the five people they are closest to. Everyone in a person's life acts as a mirror to some part of themselves. We become like the people we spend the most time with. Do the people closest to you reflect who you want to be? If not, it's time to make some changes in your relationship environment.

Mary Kay Ash, founder of Mary Kay Cosmetics, was asked, "What is the key to success in business?" Without hesitation, she responded, "Make your people feel important." One of the best ways to build relationships with those we want to be closer to is by expressing appreciation. She was known for sending out heartfelt thank-you notes.

Do just one little extraordinary activity each day, and you will create an *extraordinary* business and life. What kinds of *extra*ordinary things might you do? One of my favorite daily habits is to send an unexpected card—a note of thanks, encouragement, or just a "thinking of you" card. It's amazing what a difference this makes in building relationships. I begin each day by sending a card of gratitude to whoever is on my mind. It sets a positive tone for my whole day, and we never know when there won't be a tomorrow for someone we care about. I learned this powerful lesson when my father died. That's why it's so important to express love and gratitude today and nurture the relationships we have right now.

In music, the relationships of notes played or sung together create melody and harmony. If you think that one person is too insignificant to have an impact on your life, imagine a favorite song with one note missing throughout the piece. How would it sound if that note was never played or expressed throughout the song? Each note plays an important role in a song, just like certain people play an important role in our lives.

Now imagine a song that you know really well. Exchange one note of the piece with a different note so that each time that note appears, the wrong note is played or sung in its place. This would be very disruptive to your listening experience.

As with "wrong" notes in a song, certain relationships in your life can be very disruptive. Do an audit of your closest relationships with family, friends, and professional associations. Get clear about who is positive and supportive and who is neutral or negative and damaging for you to spend time with. This will help you invest time with relationships more wisely. Just because someone is related to you or has been your friend or colleague for a long time does not give them license to pollute your life with their toxicity.

A friend of mine used to go home for Thanksgiving dinner, and each year his mother would be critical of him at the dinner table. As a result, he dreaded going home for Thanksgiving. One year when his mother invited him for dinner, he accepted her invitation on one condition. He would no longer tolerate being criticized by her at the dinner table. When he showed up for Thanksgiving dinner, his mother started in with her critical remarks. He got up from the table and left the house. Several years passed before he accepted his mother's invitation to Thanksgiving dinner. When he finally returned, she never criticized him again.

I share my friend's story because it is a powerful illustration of how important it is for us to take responsibility for our own emotional and mental health. My friend made a request and his mother chose not to honor his boundaries, so it became his responsibility to enforce them. If you have negative people in your life—even if they are blood relatives—it is your responsibility to limit your contact with them or to at least walk away when they are not treating you with respect.

Remember Jack Canfield's number one success principle: take 100 percent responsibility for your life.

The Relationship Environment is very much like notes in a song. The notes can be harmonious or dissonant, repetitive or absent. The good news is that when you are the composer, you can rewrite a song to create the harmonies you choose.

Relationships Environment Upgrade Example

Upgrades desired

- Minimize the time I spend with (name of person or people).
- Nurture my relationships with (name of people).

Actions to be taken by when

- With calls or e-mails, let (name of person) know that I have set some goals, and in order to achieve them, I will not be available like I used to be.
- Send cards of appreciation to (name of person or people) each month.

6. **Network Environment:** greater community, strategic partners, customers, professional connections, social networks

> *Wherever we're going, we all need the help of others to get there.*
> *Don't ever be afraid to ask for what you need.*
>
> *—Harvey Mackay*

As your goals change, your network must evolve and grow. How can you team up with others to create a supportive and thriving network? Are you networked with people who pull you up or who push you down?

In music, we "network" groups of notes together using chords to create harmony. These networks of notes support each other and are a vital part of how we experience the performance of a song.

When several people get together to support each other toward achieving their goals, it's called a mastermind group. When several people get together and they have negative attitudes and negative minds, it's called a landmine group. They'll blow up your dreams and tell you all the reasons why you will fail! Surround yourself with people who support and encourage you.

If you are not currently in a mastermind group, consider joining or creating one. Choose the group carefully. For more information about mastermind groups, check out Jack Canfield's book *The Success Principles: How to Get from Where You Are to Where You Want to Be.* He provides an entire chapter that offers great tips about how to create and run a successful mastermind group.

In sports, we are taught to challenge the best players we can find because in doing so, our skill set will improve. In other words, network with those who are doing what you want to do, and soon you'll be doing it too.

If you are the role model that everyone looks up to in your network, it's time to upgrade your network—get out of your comfort zone—and spend some time with people you aspire to be like. If you are always comfortable, you are not growing. There are plenty of people who are ready and willing to support and assist you. Just remember to do the same for others when it's your turn to help.

As you build your network, it's important to collect and record information about each person. Do not rely on your memory for this. Whether you use paper (a Rolodex or an index card system) or an electronic contact manager, record the following information for each person:

- Name, mailing address, phone, e-mail, web address, etc.
- Birthday (so you can mail them a birthday card each year on their special day)

 KATHY PAAUW

- Where, when, and how you met them
- Anything interesting you learned about them (hobbies, special interests or skills, family information, career/business information, goals, challenges, etc.). This is very important to make a note of as it will help you remember topics important to them—a crucial element to building a relationship.
- Dated record of all follow-up contact you've made (call, e-mail, card, letter, etc.)

The size of your *network* determines the size of your *net worth* when you cultivate relationships. Most people attend networking events and then never follow up with the people they've just met. Make it a goal to meet two new people every day and add them to your contacts. Do this five days a week, fifty-two weeks a year, and that's 520 new people you'll add to your contact manager each year! As you live your life, you'll naturally meet new people. Make a point of getting their contact information and then keep in touch in a meaningful way.

The Pareto principle (the 80/20 rule) is important to consider when planning follow-up with your network. The next chapter provides more information about how to apply the 80/20 rule.

In reality you will actively stay in touch with 20 percent of your contacts at any given time. Having *quality* information that is current, accurate, and easy to access is important. My top 20 percent receives the following from me:

- Cards (birthday, holiday, appreciation, encouragement, congratulations etc.)
- Phone calls to check in and see how they are doing and how I can support them
- E-mails or Web links containing information I've come across that I thought would be helpful or meaningful to them
- Occasional meetings for coffee, breakfast, or lunch to learn more about them and their needs

For the other 80 percent, you'll need a good system to handle *quantity*. You need to stay connected in a way that does not require a lot of effort on your part. I stay connected with the other 80 percent in the following ways:

- birthday and holiday greeting cards (not e-cards)
- electronic newsletters/e-zines or e-mails sent to people in my network (no mailings to strangers)
- social media sites like Facebook and LinkedIn

No matter where I go, I always carry some of my own business cards. I also carry some "blank" business cards with me in the event that someone I meet does not have a business card with them. Here is what my blank cards look like:

```
Name________________________________________

Address_____________________________________

       _____________________________________

City, State, Zip____________________________

Phone(    )_________________________________

Email_______________________________________

Birthday (month/day)________________________
```

The back of this card is blank for jotting down personal notes about interests, affiliations, connections, family, accomplishments, goals, or anything else I want to remember about the person I've just met. This gets recorded in the "notes" section of my contact manager. These notes become a key part of my success in building relationships. Although I don't have great memory recall, my ability to access my notes would lead people to think otherwise!

Network Environment Upgrade Example

Upgrades desired

- Meet new people who can serve as role models or mentors to me.
- Focus 80 percent of my relationship-building time on the 20 percent of people who can help me stretch and grow professionally.
- Attract more referrals. Don't *ask* for them, *deserve* them!
- Pay it forward by helping others in my network.

Actions to be taken by when

- Join (name of group or association) by (date).
- Limit my time to no more than thirty minutes a day on social media networking, e-mail, web surfing, and other potential time wasters. Connect only with those with whom I have a clear purpose for connecting.
- In everything that I do, show up in *service*: give to give, not to get!
- Build my network by adding a new contact each day to my contact manager. Send a "nice to meet you" card after the first meeting. Stay in touch by occasionally sending helpful information or offering support.

7. Financial Environment: money (income, expenses), investments, budgeting

> *Wealth is measured by the richness of your life experience today*
> *plus the number of days into the future that you have the*
> *capacity to continue living at that level of experience.*

> —*Robert Kiyosaki, The Business of the 21st Century*

Nearly anything you do will be affected by your financial situation. How healthy is your financial life? If you don't know, it may be time to take your head out of the sand and find out how you're really doing. It is important that you have a realistic picture of your current financial health. Far too many people have lived on easy-to-get credit and have dug a deep hole because they were not paying attention.

In musical terms, finances represent the note value. One thing that makes music interesting is that not all notes have the same value. Some notes are played or sung for a short duration of time, and some are longer. If you were to compose a song, you would need to understand the different kinds of note and rest values.

Although you need to understand the facts about your current financial situation, it is also vital that you visualize the future you desire. What thoughts, habits, and actions are required to move you in the direction of achieving financial freedom?

One huge influence over your Financial Environment is your Memetics. How often do you say to yourself, "I can't afford it"? That may be a motif in your life. In *Secrets of the Millionaire Mind*, T. Harv Eker notes that each person possesses a "money blueprint"—an internal script for dealing with money—that comprises the lessons we learned in childhood. Most of us have carried those blueprints into adulthood. This is what keeps some people stuck at a certain income level—the money blueprint is set low. This is also what enables Donald Trump to lose millions of dollars and then earn it right back—his money blueprint is set very high.

Will Smith—famous actor, producer, and multimillionaire—was recently asked by Oprah, "How does it feel to be rich?" His answer may surprise you! He confided that at the end of the day, he doesn't feel rich. He still feels poor! Will Smith cannot shake the way he felt growing up—poor and always struggling for money. He routinely gets anxious and fearful that he's going to lose everything. Will's dad taught him to always work hard. As a result, he has a tremendous work ethic, but he never learned how to feel abundance in his life. Even with all his success and wealth, his mind perpetuates an internal state of "not enough." His money blueprint is set to "poor and struggling."

Those of us in network marketing have another kind of blueprint that is important to be aware of—our MLM (Multi-Level Marketing) blueprint. Kody Bateman has written an excellent book called *MLM Blueprint*, which helps you explore how you feel and what you believe about network marketing as a business model. His book also provides a process to help you overcome any negative MLM blueprint that you might have. Without a positive MLM blueprint, financial freedom will elude you.

During my senior year of college, I joined a well-known network marketing company. As a struggling college student, I was barely able to come up with the money for tuition, room, and board; so it was a real stretch for me to find additional funds to start my own network marketing business. Despite that, I was excited by the promise of doing some up-front work to build a business and then getting paid for a lifetime.

After I became a distributor, I was told that I needed to stock products if I wanted to be successful. Although it was a real stretch for me, I worked extra hours in another job to have the funds so I could do what I was taught. Unfortunately, I never made a dime from my short stint with this network marketing company,

                    KATHY PAAUW

and my dorm room closet was filled with products I could not sell. When I cancelled my distributorship with that company, I had decided that network marketing did not work and I never wanted to do another "one of those" again. To say that my MLM blueprint was low would be an understatement!

Over the years, I was invited to look at many different network marketing opportunities, and I always politely said, "No, that's not for me." Twenty-five years later, in 2005, a friend invited me to look at a network marketing company I had never heard of before. This time the company was a perfect fit for me. I loved their products, culture, values, and the people it attracted. I was a little leery because it was "one of those MLMs," but I was so passionate about the company's offerings that I knew I would tell others about it, whether I made any money at it or not. I was also interested in ways to leverage my time and generate passive income, so I decided to sign up as a distributor.

This time, my decision had a very different outcome. What was the difference? I was never passionate about the offerings of the company I signed up with twenty-five years ago. I have tremendous passion for the company I am with today and the work that I do now, so I can lead with my heart. Passion is essential to success. I had also done a lot of personal development work, and I am a different person today than I was in 1980.

Examining my own MLM blueprint, I discovered some areas in my belief system that still needed to be upgraded. Working through some limiting beliefs has been a vital part of building my thriving team. I have shifted from not wanting to be a part of *any* network marketing company to *only* wanting to invest time building financial freedom through a network marketing business model.

As you change your blueprint and learn how to allow the flow of money into your life, you may benefit from tapping into some expertise in how to leverage the money you have by making wise investments. I encourage you to seek the advice of a trusted professional who does not have ulterior motives for how to invest your money. (Some will make recommendations based on what kind of commissions they will earn off your investment transactions.) Even if you don't have much to work with, start small and build from there.

Financial Environment Upgrade Example

Upgrades desired

- Assess my financial health.
- Upgrade my MLM blueprint.

Actions to be taken by when

- Identify all assets by (date).
- Identify all debt by (date).
- Find out my credit score by (date).
- Create a realistic budget by (date).
- Read *MLM Blueprint* and do the exercises in the accompanying workbook.

8. **Physical Environment:** places, sounds, lighting, furnishings, tangible objects

Does your physical space inspire you? It's important to create space that nurtures and stimulates you on every level and helps you express your true personality and flair.

In a musical composition, the physical environment represents things that your senses pick up on, such as the tempo and dynamics of a song. These elements have a huge effect on the listener's mood. The same is true when you make adjustments to any physical environment you spend much time in, such as your home, office, or car.

In 1995, I opened my own consulting business to help people organize their work and home environments. My first year in business, I loved successfully transforming a client's home office environment from chaos and disarray to calm and productive. Several months after completing my work with a client, I would check back with them only to find that the vast majority of them were not maintaining the systems we had worked so hard to put in place.

Some of my colleagues reminded me that this was "job security" since these clients needed me to keep coming back to help them "get organized" again.

Since my goal was to help a client create and maintain a productive environment without becoming dependent on me, the "Band-Aid" business model felt very much out of integrity. I soon came to realize that organizing a client's physical environment without first clarifying their priorities was like rearranging deck chairs on the Titanic!

I started using the metaphor of an iceberg to describe the work of getting organized. The tip of the iceberg represents the physical environment that we can see and organize. The part under the waterline (the biggest part) represents the mental part of being organized—being clear about priorities and organizing one's schedule, space, and mind around those priorities. I realized that I needed some additional skills to assist my clients with the mental part of getting organized, so I became a certified professional and personal coach, and I began combining skills from both of these separate professions.

I recall one client in particular (I'll call her Jan), who invited me into her home to help her get organized. One thing I learned early on as a consultant was the importance of discovering who "owned" the problem. Initially, it sounded like Jan's husband owned the problem as he was the one who had suggested she hire me to help organize their house. But my work would be with her, not with him. I knew that if she was not motivated to solve the "problem," any work I did with her would not have lasting results. My initial sense was that Jan did not care one way or the other. I was there to appease her husband's wishes. I probed to find out if she had any personal motivation to organize and declutter their home.

Jan took me into a room that was literally filled (floor to ceiling) with boxes and piles of things. Although it was difficult to see it, in the middle of the room was a very large table, piled high with just about everything you could imagine. I asked Jan what the purpose was for the room. She told me that many years ago, she had been a quilter—something she loved doing. I asked her what stopped her from quilting if it brought her so much joy. She said that she had stopped quilting because she did not have any space to work in. The large table in the middle of this room had been a perfect space for her work, but that was years ago, and she could not imagine ever reclaiming that space. I told her if she wanted to quilt again, we could work together to make that happen. Before my eyes, I saw Jan transform from being an unmotivated bystander to becoming a highly-motivated participant in decluttering and organizing their home, starting with the room that contained her quilting table.

Organizing your time and space without working from a foundation that is based on your priorities and passions is not meaningful and the results will not last.

In section 3 of this book, I'll provide some tips and tools to assist you with decluttering your schedule, space, and mind so you can stay focused on what's most important.

Physical Environment Upgrade Example

Upgrades desired

- Create a clutter-free office that inspires me.
- Do my creative work in a room with a window that provides a view of nature.

Actions to be taken by when

- Take Kathy Paauw's next Buried in Paper free webinar so I can learn how to make quick decisions about paper and information as it comes in.
- Set up a tickler file system by (date) and commit to using my new decision-making process daily.
- Identify a creative retreat space by (date) for doing my weekly planning.

9. **Nature Environment:** outdoors, beauty, seasons, cycle of life

Our spirits are so lifted by flowers, a beautiful rainbow, a breathtaking night sky, or a walk in a lush forest. We are drawn to the beautiful views of snowcapped mountains, a field of tulips in bloom, or the amazing colors of fall along a country road.

Oftentimes we hear music in nature. Imagine the symphony of sounds created by a spring rain, crashing waves on a beach, the mating call of a bird, a pond of croaking frogs, chirping crickets at dusk, the roar of a lion, or bellowing cows at feeding time. Nature is filled with sounds of dissonance and resolution, calm and chaos, danger and peace. All of nature serves as a mirror of our own lives.

Studies have shown that our levels of psychological and physiological stress are significantly influenced by our natural surroundings. Nature is widely used as therapy for people who are suffering from physical and mental health problems. Research done in the Netherlands and Japan revealed that people living close to green ambience live longer and enjoy greater health. A Swedish study concluded that office workers who viewed greenery through their office windows had lower stress levels during their workday. Studies from Germany and Australia found that plant ecosystems work as powerful air purifiers.

Our deep and compelling desire for a connection with nature has the potential to be a constant source of inspiration as well as a boost to our physical and mental health. No matter what else is going on in our lives, connection to nature can restore our sense of wonder and awaken our senses.

Nature Environment Upgrade Example

Upgrade desired

- Enjoy a deeper connection with nature.

Action to be taken by when

- Go to the beach or the mountains one weekend each month with (name of person).

All Nine Environments

Success can be achieved and sustained only when all nine environments are working together to support you. Change your environments and you'll change your life. Changing only one or two of them does not have the same impact!

I'll share a personal example of how all the environments are so connected. The purpose of sharing such a deeply personal story is to help you understand that what you do in one environment affects all the other environments.

For decades I dealt with some serious issues with two family members. My brother had a drug-and-alcohol addiction, and my mother had been his "enabler" for his entire adult life. He had been living in the family room of my mother's one-bedroom apartment for a long time. Despite her desire to see him live a clean life, she did not have the strength to practice "tough love" by moving him out and allowing him to live with the consequences of his own choices. Many years prior, I had decided to set some firm boundaries to protect myself from getting pulled into their unhealthy codependent relationship. For as long as I could remember, I had prayed that my mother would stop supporting my brother's addictions and that he would become motivated to get whatever help he needed to stay clean and sober and live a productive life.

Finally, the day that I had been praying for came. My mother called to tell me that she was ready to start practicing "tough love" with my brother and was no longer supporting him, but she did not think she had the strength to stick to her plan on her own. My mother moved in with my family so we could be there to support her when he sought her out for help. Several weeks later, I discovered that my brother had been living at my mother's apartment—only two miles from our home—and she was still supporting him. She had been hiding this from us the whole time she was living under our roof. When I found out what was going on, I was furious! She had crossed some boundaries and violated our trust. We had supported her under false pretense.

I became nonfunctional as I allowed myself to get drawn into the drama. My relationship with my mother quickly deteriorated, and I asked her to move back to her apartment. I judged her harshly for hiding the truth from me to gain my support. I was emotionally spiraling downward and could not see how to pull myself out of it.

Then I remembered the nine environments model. I took out a piece of paper and listed each one. I also wrote down what I wanted to upgrade in each environment.

Beginning with Memetic, I wrote down some old beliefs I had allowed to creep in from my childhood: "You're not lovable . . . you don't deserve . . ." My self-talk was "proving" these beliefs to be true as I found evidence to convince myself that my mother loved my brother more than me.

I proceeded to examine the other eight environments:

- **Relationships**: Not only was my relationship with my mother in bad shape, but also I had been very irritable and short fused with my husband and daughter.
- **Network**: I was completely disengaged from my network. I was not connecting with anyone, and this was affecting my business.
- **Financial**: I was having trouble concentrating on my work responsibilities, and that was affecting my bottom line.
- **Body**: I was not getting much sleep, had stopped exercising, and was eating a lot of high carb comfort foods (chocolate and potatoes). I was exhausted.
- **Physical**: I had piles of papers all over my office (delayed decisions) because I was having trouble concentrating on my work. The clutter was weighing me down.
- **Nature**: I felt completely cut off from nature. I was unaware of anything outside of my immediate surroundings.
- **Self**: My skills and talents were going to waste. I was barely present for my coaching and consulting appointments with my clients or for training and coaching calls with my team members. I was not making any kind of meaningful contribution because I was so busy having a "pity party" for myself. I had stopped singing in choir at church.
- **Spiritual**: My spiritual practices had gone out the window. One of my standard practices is expressing gratitude at the beginning of each day. I had forgotten what I was grateful for and had stopped sending my daily gratitude cards to others.

I began to identify action steps I could take to upgrade each of the nine environments, beginning with Memetic. With the help of my personal coach, I uncovered a hidden belief that I had developed as a young adult: "I have to be right, powerful, and superior to survive."

Once I became consciously aware of this belief, I asked myself if it served me to continue believing it. I realized that this belief would not support the kind of relationships I wanted to have with others. Just being conscious of its existence reduced its power over me.

I chose to replace that belief with one that would allow for a healthier relationship with those I care about: "I am a generous servant leader."

As I worked through the other eight environments, I identified action steps I could take to upgrade each one. Taking conscious action helped me reverse the downward spiral I had been experiencing. I took steps to align my life with my new belief: I am a generous servant leader.

FREEDOM CHALLENGE

With a highlighter, identify your level of satisfaction with each of the environments on the wheel below. For example, if you are 20 percent satisfied with an environment, color in 20 percent of that wedge on the wheel, coloring from the middle outward. If you are 90 percent satisfied, color in 90 percent of the wedge. For Memetic, color in the percentage of the circle that conveys your level of satisfaction.

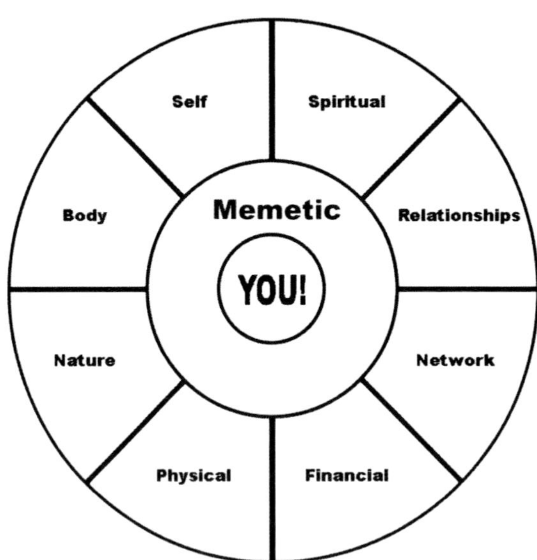

If this was a wheel on your car, you can see how smooth or how bumpy the ride would be, based on how you colored in your wheel!

     KATHY PAAUW

Now it's time to identify what you are currently tolerating in each of your nine environments and *what you desire to be, do, or have instead*. Then *identify specific actions you will take* to upgrade each environment, and indicate the *date by when you will have taken these actions*. Refer back to the examples provided earlier in this chapter if you have trouble getting started.

Memetic Environment (beliefs, values, ideas, thoughts, frameworks)

Below are some questions to help you get clear about what you are tolerating in your Memetic Environment:

1. Do I choose my beliefs rather than simply accepting what I learned or heard?

2. Does my current belief system support my growth and development?

3. Do I challenge my old beliefs that no longer serve me?

4. Am I clear about my core values (absolutes that are not negotiable)?

5. Do I stretch beyond my own comfort zone to learn and grow?

6. Do I limit the amount of negative news, radio, and television I am exposed to?

7. Do I carefully select "positive programming" for my brain?

8. Do I use empowering language regularly (I choose to . . .) versus victim language (I should . . ., I gotta . . ., I have to . . .)?

9. Do I maintain healthy boundaries with others?

10. Does the "lens" through which I view my life support me in moving toward my intentions?

Upgrades desired:

➤

➤

➤

Actions to be taken by when:

>
>
>

Body Environment (physical appearance, health, energy)

Below are some questions to help you get clear about what you are tolerating in your Body Environment:

1. Do I get exercise daily (cardio and strength training)?

2. Do I nourish my body with healthy foods and avoid overeating?

3. Do I stay adequately hydrated?

4. Do I get regular medical and dental checkups and follow the advice of professionals who care for me?

5. Do I get enough sleep?

6. Do I have an abundance of energy?

7. Do I maintain a healthy weight, blood pressure, cholesterol level, etc.?

8. Do I limit my alcohol and caffeine intake?

9. Do I abuse any drugs (legal or illegal) or have any addictions that need attention?

10. Is my selection of clothing and accessories a reflection of who I am and who I choose to project?

Upgrades desired:

>
>
>

Actions to be taken by when:

>
>
>

Self Environment (personality, temperament, character, gifts, talents, strengths)

Below are some questions to help you get clear about what you are tolerating in your Self Environment:

1. Am I aware of my self-talk? Do I avoid victim language (I should . . ., I gotta . . ., I have to . . .)?

2. Do I know my strongest skills, talents, and strengths and use them as leverage to maximize my success?

3. Do I maintain strong boundaries in my life when with people who could violate them?

4. Do I take 100 percent responsibility for my own life versus blaming others or justifying when things don't go as I wanted them to?

5. Do I live an authentic life?

6. Do I appropriately display emotions?

7. Do I have a positive self-image or self-esteem?

8. Do I inspire others in the way that I live my life?

9. Do I honor priorities?

10. Do I live in integrity by keeping my word to myself and others?

Upgrades desired:

>
>
>

Actions to be taken by when:

- ➤
- ➤
- ➤

Spiritual Environment (deep connections)

Below are some questions to help you get clear about what you are tolerating in your Spiritual Environment:

1. Do I feel connected to my own spiritual intuition?

2. Do I feel connected to a higher power?

3. Do I feel connected to other human beings and to nature?

4. Do I feel the freedom to examine beliefs I was raised with and then choose the right path for me?

5. Do I honor and respect other people's spiritual beliefs even if I disagree with them?

6. Am I committed to a daily spiritual practice?

7. Do my spiritual practices enable me to give of my time and talents to others?

8. Do I get my energy from negative points of power such as apathy, grief, fear, lust, control, overwhelm, clutter, addictions, manipulation, and anger *or* from positive points of power such as love, truth, courageousness, beauty, gratitude, and peace?

9. Do I regularly practice "letting go" of my attachments to outcomes?

10. Do I express gratitude daily for what I have, regardless of how my day went?

Upgrades desired:

>
>
>

Actions to be taken by when:

>
>
>

Relationships Environment (family, close friends, colleagues, support personnel)

Below are some questions to help you get clear about what you are tolerating in your Relationship Environment:

1. Are my relationships built on trust, mutual respect, honesty, and integrity?

2. Do I have any unresolved issues with important people in my life?

3. Do I maintain any relationships with people who are damaging, draining, or abusive?

4. Do the people who I spend the most time with support me and bring out the best in me?

5. Do I feel comfortable being authentic with people?

6. Do I forgive others who have wronged me?

7. Do I apologize when I have wronged someone else?

8. Do I engage in gossip?

9. Do I regularly experience laughter and joy?

10. Do I freely give and receive love and gratitude on a regular basis?

Upgrades desired:

>
>
>

Actions to be taken by when:

>
>
>

Network Environment (greater community, strategic partners, customers, professional connections, social networks)

Below are some questions to help you get clear about what you are tolerating in your Network Environment:

1. Is my network comprised mostly of "givers" or "takers"?

2. When I network, am I giving to give or giving to get? Am I giving with no attachment to the outcome or no expectation of return? Do I add value to the other person?

3. Do I network locally and globally in a way that supports my goals? Do I have a broad enough and diverse enough network that I can access people I do not yet know through the people I do know?

4. When people see me coming, are they excited to see me or are they doing everything they can to avoid me?

5. Am I able to quickly and easily find information I need through my network?

6. Do I belong to mastermind groups that support my need to learn and grow?

7. Do I leverage social networks online?

8. Do I express a genuine curiosity about people I meet?

     KATHY PAAUW

9. Am I capturing contact information so I can creatively and intentionally keep the relationship growing over time, or am I relying on my memory?

10. Do I stay connected on a regular basis with people I have met through my networking? Am I remembered?

Upgrades desired:

>
>
>

Actions to be taken by when:

>
>
>

Financial Environment (income, expenses, budgeting, investments)

Below are some questions to help you get clear about what you are tolerating in your Financial Environment:

1. Do my finances allow me to be at choice in my life, or are my decisions controlled by money?

2. Am I able to retire when I want to?

3. Do I have any credit card debt?

4. Am I a good manager of my finances?

5. Do I know the "bottom line" of my finances at any given time?

6. Do I have a good credit score?

7. Does money flow freely into my life? Do I have a high MLM blueprint?

8. Have I leveraged my money through smart investments?

9. Am I working with competent and trusted financial advisors, CPAs, and other financial professionals I need to help me with decisions and actions I need to take?

10. Do I have adequate coverage for medical, auto, home, life, and disability insurance?

Upgrades desired:

➢
➢
➢

Actions to be taken by when:

➢
➢
➢

Physical Environment (places, sounds, lighting, furnishings, tangible objects)

Below are some questions to help you get clear about what you are tolerating in your Physical Environment:

1. Does my physical environment at work inspire me?

2. Does my physical environment at home inspire me and bring me joy?

3. Do my environments I spend time in (office, home, car, etc.) reflect who I am and help me feel "at home" when I am there?

4. Is my physical environment clean and clutter free?

5. Is my physical environment welcoming to others? Do I freely invite people into my space?

6. Are the "tools" I regularly use in good working order?

7. Do I have good lighting?

8. Do the sounds around me support my work? Do I need to add or reduce sound?

9. Do I have comfortable furnishings that enable me to work without feeling physical stress?

10. Is my environment organized so I can find what I need when I need it?

Upgrades desired:

➢
➢
➢

Actions to be taken by when:

➢
➢
➢

Nature Environment (outdoors, beauty, seasons, cycle of life)

Below are some questions to help you get clear about what you are tolerating in your Nature Environment:

1. Do I live in the geographical location of my choice (in the climate of my choosing, with the kinds of activities I enjoy doing)?

2. Do I connect with nature to inspire me and to restore myself spiritually, mentally, and physically?

3. Do I take time to fully appreciate the natural beauty around me wherever I am?

4. Do I schedule time to enjoy the great outdoors in ways that nourish me?

5. Is my yard (or area surrounding my home) to my liking?

6. Do I take time to enjoy the senses (sights, sounds, smells, touch) that nature offers?

7. Do I live in a safe environment?

8. Do I utilize natural resources in a responsible way?

9. Do I recycle and contribute to building sustainable environments?

10. Do I treat other living creatures with respect?

Upgrades desired:

>
>
>

Actions to be taken by when: _______________

>
>
>

PART THREE

Support Your Path to Freedom

This section of the book offers some tools and processes that are designed to help you be more productive and keep you focused on what's most important.

Stephen Covey wrote a best seller called *The Seven Habits of Highly Effective People*. The third of his seven habits was so important that he wrote another book called *First Things First*. These books have served as the cornerstone for much of my work as a productivity consultant and a life coach. I have taught many workshops using some of Covey's tools, which I will share with you in chapters 7, 8, and 12 (shared with permission from Franklin Covey). I have observed hundreds of people transform their lives by applying Covey's tools.

I'll include my own narrative comments and stories to help you understand the value of applying these tools to your life. Even if you are already familiar with some of the tools, I invite you to read this section of the book with fresh eyes and consider how this will support you on your path to freedom.

CHAPTER 6

Put First Things First

In 1906, Italian economist Vilfredo Pareto created a mathematical formula to describe the unequal distribution of wealth in his country, observing that 80 percent of the land in Italy was owned by 20 percent of the population. After Pareto made his observation and created his formula, many others observed similar phenomena in their own areas of expertise.

In the 1940s, quality management pioneer Dr. Joseph Juran recognized a universal principle which he called the "vital few and trivial many." A lack of precision on Juran's part made it appear that he was applying Pareto's observations about economics to his own observations. As a result, Juran's observation of the "vital few and trivial many" became known as *Pareto principle*—commonly known today as the *80/20 rule*.

The *80/20 rule* means that with anything—time, resources, space, etc.—a few (20 percent) are vital and many (80 percent) are trivial.

Here are some examples of how we can apply the *80/20 rule*. See if you recognize any that hold true for you.

- Eighty percent of what you store is never referenced again; the other 20 percent is what you use regularly (this includes paper, clothes, and other tangible items).
- Twenty percent of your products account for 80 percent of product sales.
- Eighty percent of your measurable results will come from 20 percent of the items on your "to-do" list.
- Twenty percent of your team members produce 80 percent of your results.
- Eighty percent of your managerial concerns are caused by 20 percent of the same recurring problems.
- Eighty percent of customer complaints are about the same 20 percent of your products or services.

The value of the *Pareto principle* is that it reminds us to focus on what matters most. Focus 80 percent of your time and energy on the 20 percent of your work that is really important since only those top 20 percent activities will yield 80 percent of the results you desire. If something isn't going to get done, make sure it's part of the "trivial many" (80 percent) activities that you are neglecting.

Today we have more responsibilities and choices pulling at us than ever before. *Consistent application of this rule will lead to dramatically improved productivity.* While the rule is not an absolute, you can use it as a guide to determine if you are truly focusing on the 20 percent (the vital few) or the 80 percent (the trivial many).

The world does not pay you for what you know. Many people *say* they want greater success, and yet they do not take action! They analyze, plan, study, organize, talk; but they don't take action! Even if the action you take is just a small step, take action!

True progress results from a consistent focus on the top 20 percent of your most important action steps. Note that 20 percent of an eight-hour workday is only ninety-six minutes!

There are three common challenges that get in the way of putting your *first things first*:

- *Being clear about your priorities*: who you want to be and what you want to do (goal setting)
- *Organizing your time*: identifying specific activities that will help you accomplish your goals and stay focused on your priorities (planning and scheduling)
- *Executing the plan*: following through with your intention and doing what you say you will do (accountability)

You may find that you are challenged by a combination of the above or that you are really good at two areas, but you consistently fall short in a third one. *Awareness* is the first step. *Changing habits* is the second. Your habits speak louder than your excuses! Whatever actions you take today will determine your tomorrow. This section of the book will provide you with the tools to help you change and maintain new habits.

 KATHY PAAUW

Most people don't plan to fail; they fail to plan. Planning is important because it provides a road map to help you accomplish your goals. If you don't have a plan and you don't know where you are going, any road will take you there.

Planning can take many forms—daily, weekly, quarterly, annual, five-year, and long-range planning. For small business owners, I consider quarterly, weekly, and daily planning to be the most important.

A quarterly plan provides a bigger picture view of your intentions and goals. A weekly plan enables you to make necessary adjustments to your quarterly plan. A daily plan enables you to fine-tune your weekly plan so you can address challenges and opportunities that you did not know about when you initially planned your week.

The next two chapters will help you clarify priorities and plan your investment of time around those priorities.

FREEDOM CHALLENGE

Identify your top 20 percent activities that will yield 80 percent of the results you desire in each of these areas of your life:

- Career/work—paid or volunteer
- Relationships—family and close friends
- Health—physical, mental, spiritual
- Prosperity—finances, lifestyle, time, possessions
- Environment—personal, local, global

If you work a forty-hour workweek, block out ninety minutes a day for Pareto time. (If you work more or less, do the math to figure out what 20 percent of that time is.) Honor that time by focusing on the top 20 percent of activities (actions) you have identified to be most important for accomplishing your goals.

Which of these provide the greatest obstacle to putting your *first things first?* Circle the one that challenges you the most. Carve out time to complete the worksheets that correspond with the challenge area(s) for you.

- Being clear about your priorities: chapters 1-4 of this book
- Organizing your time: chapters 5-8 of this book
- Executing the plan: chapters 9-15 of this book

 KATHY PAAUW

CHAPTER 7

Urgency vs. Importance

The main thing is to keep the main thing the main thing.

—Stephen Covey, First Things First

In network marketing, unless the activity is something that will ultimately produce team volume, it is not important to the growth of your business. It's easy for us to get lured into activities that are time wasters that do not build the business. Get clear about what your daily, weekly, and monthly core activities are; and it will be easier for you to make decisions about what's important and what is not important to do.

One of the most valuable planning tools I have found is Stephen Covey's time management matrix. This is a great tool for helping you evaluate your investment of time from a bigger picture view.

Generally speaking, we are an *urgency-addicted* society. We tend to focus on that which is urgent—whether the activity is important or not. I can easily get off track if I allow my incoming e-mail, phone calls, or text messages to take precedence over other activities that are more important to me. It's so easy to make urgency the dominant factor and completely lose track of what's most important.

If you struggle with a strong urgency mind-set, I guarantee that you will feel more satisfied and fulfilled when you take steps to focus your time and energy on *what's most important* and avoid those activities that are *not important* to you.

To help you make better decisions about how you spend your time, Covey has created the following matrix, which breaks time into four quadrants:

Time Management Matrix
Stephen Covey, *First Things First*
(shared with permission from Franklin Covey)

	Urgent	Not Urgent
Important	**I** (MANAGE) • Crisis • Medical Emergencies • Pressing Problems • Deadline-driven Projects • Last-minute Preparations for Scheduled Activities **Quadrant of Necessity**	**II** (FOCUS) • Preparation/Planning • Prevention • Values Clarification • Exercise • Relationship Building • True Recreation/Relaxation **Quadrant of Quality & Personal Leadership**
Not Important	**III** (AVOID) • Interruptions, Some Calls • Some Mail & Reports • Some Meetings • Many "Pressing" Matters • Many Popular Activities **Quadrant of Deception**	**IV** (AVOID) • Trivia, Busywork • Junk Mail • Some Phone Messages/Email • Time Wasters • Escape Activities • Viewing Mindless TV Shows **Quadrant of Waste**

I'll review each of these quadrants to help you better understand the power of applying this model to your life.

Quadrant 1: Quadrant of Necessity (Q1)

This quadrant represents activities that are necessary for you to focus on because they are *urgent* (time sensitive) *and important* to you.

We tend to focus on Q1 activities because they are urgent, and the need to do these activities makes itself known to us. These activities are hard to ignore

                    KATHY PAAUW

because our life experiences have taught us that when we ignore Q1 activities, we get into trouble.

If you have a lot of Q1 activities in your life and you find yourself frequently saying, "I have to . . ." or "I gotta . . ."—victim language—it may be time for you to reconsider what you are doing. An estimated 80 percent of the population puts themselves into a self-imposed prison cell on a regular basis. We forfeit our freedom of choice through our own thought processes. When I hear someone using victim language, I often ask them, "Do you *have* to or do you *choose* to?" There are very few things in life that you *have* to do. Yet some forfeit their ability to choose and view their options in life as limited. This generally leads to a feeling of hopelessness. If you do not feel at choice about some of your urgent and important activities, it may be time to change your focus. There are times that we truly are victims, but often this has been self-imposed by limiting our own choices.

Some urgencies—like medical emergencies—are not something we consciously choose. It's something we simply must handle. My father did not choose to have a heart attack. However, at some level, he did make a choice—by living a sedentary life and eating a high-fat, high-cholesterol diet—despite the warning bells sounded by his doctor. He'd had high blood pressure for quite some time and was not doing his part to manage his heart disease. Had he focused more time in Q2 (not urgent but important activities), doing regular exercise and eating a healthier diet, he may have avoided escalating his health management to Q1 (urgent and important) at the time of his heart attack.

For thirteen years, I chose to stay in a stressful career that I did not find fulfilling—one with a lot of Q1 activities attached to it. The more time I invested in that career path, the less at choice I felt. At one point, I took an exam to receive a special certification in my field. When I passed the exam and was certified, I felt like there was no turning back! I told myself, "I *can't* leave this field now . . . look how much I've invested in it!" And besides, I had no idea what else I could possibly do. Fear held me back until one day, the *pain of not making a change* outweighed the *fear of the unknown.*

In my years of coaching, I've found that when my clients focus on their values—what's most important to them at the core—they are more at choice and less at effect. They recognize that they have the freedom to choose based on their own values versus being influenced by limiting beliefs, circumstances, or the opinions of others.

Quadrant 2: Quadrant of Quality and Personal Leadership (Q2)

This quadrant represents activities that are *important*, but because they are *not urgent*, they are easy to put on the back burner for "when I have more time." In order to focus on these activities, one must be proactive.

The more time we spend in Q2, the more quality we add to our lives. If we neglect Q2 activities long enough, sometimes they become Q1 activities (urgent and important). For example, if your spouse came home and told you that he/she was leaving if you didn't devote more time to him/her, relationship building (generally considered Q2—not urgent but important) would probably become a Q1 (urgent and important) activity.

Unfortunately, "more time" never comes. We all get 168 hours a week. The best way to "find" more time is to reduce the amount of time you spend in Q3 and invest that time in Q2 activities instead.

Quadrant 3: Quadrant of Deception (Q3)

This quadrant represents activities that are *not important* but *urgent* (time-sensitive). Q3 is known as the quadrant of deception because we get deceived into believing that these activities are important because they are *urgent* even though we've identified these activities as *not important*.

The word "urgent" means that the activity is time sensitive or deadline driven. For example, an incoming phone call is considered urgent because the phone is ringing right now. It may or may not be important, but if you don't answer the phone now, it will stop ringing. Sometimes incoming e-mail, text messages, and Facebook posts feel urgent although they are often not important.

You'll need to say no to or renegotiate activities that are urgent but not important to you. The only exception to this would be activities that are important to someone who is important to you, so you choose to make that activity a priority even though the activity itself is not important to you. There is a huge difference between *choosing* to make something important and feeling like you *have to* do it (victim thinking).

Here's an example of when I chose to move a Q3 activity to Q1. When my daughter was little, she wanted *Goodnight Moon* read to her every single night at bedtime. Reading that same book every evening was not personally important to me, but because the *relationship* was important to me and that activity was important to her, I *chose* to make it *important* to read that book to her every night. It was *urgent* because bedtime was at a specific time.

Quadrant 4: Quadrant of Waste (Q4)

This quadrant represents activities that are *not important* and are *not urgent.*

The most common Q4 activity I've encountered in my work with busy people is *escape activities.* When the stress level gets high enough, some people escape from reality by doing activities that do not address or resolve the problem. This is considered wasteful.

Note that the same activity can fall into Q2 or Q4. If you are enjoying true recreation or you are relaxing, resting, and rejuvenating yourself, the activity falls into Q2. If you are engaged in an escape activity—doing something to avoid addressing a problem or challenge in your life—it is a Q4 activity. In other words, it's the motivation behind doing the activity that determines whether or not it is a Q2 (rejuvenating) or Q4 (escape) activity. You are the only one who can determine this.

A friend of mine loves to watch *Judge Judy* every afternoon on television. He is a top income producer and team builder in our company, and he does a great job of managing his priorities. In his case, watching this TV show is not a Q4 "escape" activity for him, but rather a Q2 "rejuvenating" activity. He does not watch much TV, but this particular show really brings him joy, and he carves out time for it every afternoon.

Many people are "urgency-addicted"—a self-destructive behavior that temporarily fills a void created by unmet needs. This type of addiction is as dangerous as other commonly recognized addictions and dependencies.

The goal is to *manage activities in Q1, focus on activities in Q2,* and *avoid activities in Q3 and Q4*—activities that you've deemed as not important. Because so many of us are urgency addicted, we tend to spend the bulk of our time in Q1 and Q3—doing activities that are *urgent and important* or *urgent but not important.*

In network marketing, unless the activity is something that will ultimately produce team volume, it is not important to the growth of your business. It's easy for us to get lured into activities that are time wasters that do not build the business. Get clear about what your daily, weekly, and monthly core activities are; and it will be easier for you to make decisions about what's important and what is not important.

Now that you have a tool to help you identify activities that are not important to you, it's time to make some conscious choices about how you spend your time in the future.

FREEDOM CHALLENGE

Create your own time management matrix:

- Draw the four quadrants on a sheet of paper as in the diagram provided.
- Review your activities and list them under the appropriate quadrants.
- Identify which activities in Q3 and Q4 you will say no to and which activities in quadrant 2 you plan to add to your weekly schedule. Remember that every time you say yes to someone or something, you are saying no to someone or something else!

The next chapter will help you plan Q2 activities into your week.

CHAPTER 8

Weekly Planning

Besides the time management matrix, my favorite planning tool is Stephen Covey's *Six Step Weekly Planning Process*. Here is the process (shared with permission from Franklin Covey):

Step 1: Connect with your vision and mission.
Step 2: Review your key roles.
Step 3: Identify your weekly goals (choices)—in writing.
Step 4: Organize your time (schedule your priorities).
Step 5: Exercise integrity in the moment of choice.
Step 6: Evaluate and learn.

I will describe this process below in greater detail. For a more in-depth look, I encourage you to read Covey's books, *The Seven Habits of Highly Effective People* and *First Things First*.

Step 1: Connect with Your Vision and Mission

> *The wind is never favorable to those who don't know where they are going.*
>
> —*Lucius Annaeus Seneca*

If you'd like a tool to help you begin drafting your mission, Franklin Covey provides a mission statement builder at *www.franklincovey.com/msb/*.

Your mission statement represents your values, vision, and purpose for your life. Only a very small percentage of the population has written a personal mission statement. Once you've written yours, begin your weekly planning time by reviewing it. This is the foundation upon which you plan your week.

As part of my coach training, I attended a three-day workshop called Living Your Vision®, and each participant drilled down deep to create their own purpose statements. It was intense work. Mine is only one sentence long, and that single sentence represents my core purpose. Here it is: *I am a divine messenger of peace, compassionately infusing balance and harmony.*

When I have difficulty making a decision, my purpose statement helps me make better choices. My statement reminds me that as one of God's divine creations, I have a responsibility to be a good steward of the gifts I have been given. My statement also reminds me of my core values—peace, balance, and harmony. When making decisions, I ask myself, "Will this move me toward promoting peace, balance, and harmony or away from it?"

I am grateful that I invested three days of my time back in 1999 to do this deeper work because it has served as a guiding light for me when I come to a crossroads or need to make a difficult decision. These values are so core to who I am that they will serve me throughout my lifetime, regardless of what I choose to do.

If you have not done this deep work of getting clear about your purpose, I invite you to do the work so you have a compass to help guide your life decisions. If you want assistance with this, you can find workshops, books, CDs, and coaches who are available to help you navigate through the process.

Step 2: Review Your Key Roles

> *The key is not to prioritize what's on your schedule,*
> *but to schedule your priorities.*
>
> —Stephen Covey

What are the most important roles in your life? Start with the four elements of self (physical, mental, spiritual, and social well-being), and then identify a *maximum of seven roles* of greatest importance to you. Planning with these roles in mind will help you stay focused on your priorities and build balance into your life.

 KATHY PAAUW

As Mother Teresa once said, "To keep the lamp burning, you have to keep putting oil in it." It's so important to take care of ourselves first. Only then are we fully available to assist others. When flying somewhere, flight attendants always remind us to put our own oxygen mask on first before assisting others. Why? Because if we lose consciousness, we won't be available to help ourselves or anyone else.

I'll share my own personal roles below as an example, including sub roles for Role 4 (Entrepreneur), so you can see how this looks.

<u>Self:</u> physical, mental, spiritual, social

Role 1: Wife

Role 2: Mother

Role 3: Family Member

Role 4: Entrepreneur ———————▶

Role 5: Friend

Role 6: Community Volunteer

Role 7: Singer

<u>Entrepreneur</u> (Role 4)
Consultant/Coach
Trainer/Speaker/Presenter/Singer
Manager/Administrator
Networker
Writer
Team Mentor / Company Leader
Lifelong Learner

Step 3: Identify Your Weekly Goals (Choices)—In Writing

What does it matter how much we do
if what we're doing isn't what matters most?

—Stephen Covey, First Things First

Think of two or three important results you want to accomplish during the coming week in each role you identified in step 2. Write this week's goals next to each role. By identifying your goals this way, you are more likely to build balance into your life.

I prefer thinking of this as weekly choices because sometimes goals can begin to feel like a "should" or a "have to" once they are set. Use whatever terminology speaks to you.

Effective goals will reflect these elements:

1. They are driven by conscience, and they align with your personal vision and mission.

2. Your focus is on the "important" rather than just the "urgent."

3. Your goals are driven by choice, not by what you "should" do.

Covey suggests that you ask yourself this question for each of your roles: *what is the most important thing I can do in this role this week to have the greatest positive impact?*

There's a difference between consciously choosing *not* to do something with a particular role and simply not getting around to doing it. As you do your planning, remind yourself of this truth: *every time I say yes to someone or something, I am saying no to someone or something else!*

Step 4: Organize Your Time (Schedule Your Priorities)

Discipline is the bridge between goals and accomplishment.

—Jim Rohn

Schedule a weekly one-hour appointment with yourself and follow this six-step planning process as you plan each week. Look at the week ahead with your written goals in front of you and schedule time to take the action required to achieve them. Be sure you are scheduling some of your quadrant 2 activities—important and not urgent—because they probably won't happen unless you carve out the time for them.

Planning tip: Be sure your calendar also includes some unscheduled time. If every minute of every day is already booked, you are setting yourself up for failure. Allow time for some unexpected but important activities when planning your week.

Tool tip: Use a weekly planner rather than a daily or monthly planner. If you use a hand-held electronic device (BlackBerry, iPhone, etc.), do your planning at a computer screen where you can see the whole week at once, and then sync your calendar with your device.

 KATHY PAAUW

Step 5: Exercise Integrity in the Moment of Choice!

*Even if you're on the right track,
you'll get run over if you just sit there.*

—*Will Rogers*

When making schedule adjustments, review your mission to help you stay on track. If something more important comes up, *reschedule* the planned activity for another time. Decisions are based on your priorities.

Be a gatekeeper—say *no* to activities or responsibilities which will derail you from living *on purpose*. Be aware of self-talk that includes victim language (should, gotta, have to). This is your life and you are in control!

Years ago I was not "exercising integrity in the moment of choice." My coach was helping me look at what was stopping me from honoring my commitment to exercise first thing in the morning, and she asked me to describe what was happening. I told her that when my alarm went off, I hit the snooze button and went back to sleep; and by the time I got up, it was time to get in the shower and get ready for my day. She asked me, "What do you say to yourself when the alarm goes off?" I said, "I have to get up and exercise!" She reflected my own language back to me. "I *have to* get up and exercise!" When I realized what I was saying to myself, I made a decision to change my self-talk.

The next morning when the alarm went off, I said to myself, "I *choose to* get up and exercise because I am committed to good health." I was amazed at what a difference my choice of words made! As long as it was something I *had to* do, I was digging my heels in and resisting it.

Step 6: Evaluate and Learn

*If you keep doing what you're doing, you'll keep getting what you're getting!
One definition of insanity is to keep doing the same things
and expecting different results.*

—*Stephen Covey*

Before you plan for the coming week, learn from what didn't work the week before. Make adjustments in your planning so you can work toward a different outcome the next week. Although this is listed as the sixth step in the process, I suggest that you move it up to step 3. In other words, review your mission and roles, then evaluate how the previous week went before making your choices for the coming week, scheduling them into your calendar, and living your week with integrity.

One of the things I love about this weekly planning process is that each week I get to start fresh. Charles Dederich once said, *"Today is the first day of the rest of your life."* If you've had a bad day or a bad week—and we all have them—remember that you'll get a fresh start tomorrow. It's not productive to steer the wheel while staring into your rearview mirror! There's tremendous power in taking a moment to learn from the past and then leaving the past in the past and moving forward.

Now that you have a weekly planning process to follow, be sure you carve out time each week to do it! One of the most common things I hear people say is, "I don't have time to plan." That's exactly why you need to plan! We all get 168 hours a week. It's not a matter of not having enough time but of not being clear about your priorities and not designating specific time in your schedule for what's most important.

Remember the 80/20 rule. Even if you waste 80 percent of your time, if you focus 20 percent of your time on the activities that you know yield the greatest results, you'll be amazed at how many of your goals you achieve.

One of the best ways to "find" time is to devote less time to the activities that are not helping you move in the direction you want to go. You are either moving toward or away from what you choose. If you skipped the Freedom Challenge in chapter 7, I invite you to go back and identify which activities in Q3 and Q4 you will say no to and which activities in Q2 you plan to add to your weekly schedule.

In Tony Rubleski's book *Mind Capture: How to Awaken Your Entrepreneurial Genius in a Time of Great Economic Change*, he says, *"The world rewards action. Until you're in motion, nothing will change. I've lost track of how many people I've met who still have their dreams, ideas, inventions and solutions buried in their minds or stuck on a shelf in their home or office collecting dust. They are imprisoned in a mental room of their own design, with four walls they've constructed which go by the names of procrastination, doubt, fear and security."*

 KATHY PAAUW

Here are some ways to reclaim some of your time so you can repurpose it and take action:

1. The Nielsen ratings tell us that statistically, the average American watches at least four hours of television a day. What if you gave up one or two of those hours and focused on your intention to build your network marketing business rather than giving into what you feel like at the moment? If you don't watch much television, perhaps you spend lots of time on the Internet or you have another activity that eats up time with very little return on your investment. Look for Q3 or Q4 activities you can cut out of your schedule so you can invest in your future by consistently building your network marketing business.

2. Ask for help. Delegate some or all the tasks which are not the best use of your time. If your budget does not allow for hiring help, barter with others or hire a local teenager who can do an adequate job for less cost than a professional.

3. Stop saying "I'll try . . ." That language is very disempowering! Either do it or don't do it! Be committed to what you say yes to, and be clear about what you say no to.

4. Set three types of goals—*minimum*, *target*, and *outrageous*. Once you get started working on the *minimum goal*, the momentum may be present for you to continue working toward your target or outrageous goal. Here is an example of how this works:

   - Minimum goal: By the end of today, I will go through one stack of papers on my desk and either toss, delegate, take action, or file it.

   - Target goal: By the end of this week, I will clear my entire desk of paper piles by tossing anything that does not enhance my life, delegating what I can, taking action on what needs my attention, or filing it away for future reference.

   - Outrageous goal: By the end of this week, I will hire someone to help me organize my entire office.

Get started now! In the next fifteen minutes, do something that will move you toward your intention.

FREEDOM CHALLENGE

Take charge of how you invest your time by doing the following activities.

1. Schedule a standing weekly appointment with yourself for weekly planning (preferably the same time each week to build it as a habit).

2. Complete all six steps of the planning process provided.

3. Identify an intention you want to get some traction on, and set minimum, target, and outrageous goals for it.

4. Here's a great exercise from Tony Rubleski's book. Below you'll find a list of mind-set habits to avoid as well as new habits to replace them with. Review the lists below and underline the top 2 areas that need to be improved upon in order to help you take consistent action.

Runner-up Mind-set Habits	**Champion Mind-set Habits**
Making excuses	Get things done on time
Easily distracted	Focused
Inconsistent	Able to hit deadlines
Disorganized and waste time	In control and efficient
Blame others	Personal responsibility
Stop learning	Learn new things each day
Engage in gossip	Look for the good in each situation
Too much TV and Internet	Limited TV and Internet time
Associate with negative people	Hang around positive people
Laziness	Fierce, passionate, and determined
Shy	Confident and assertive

CHAPTER 9

The Fortune Is in the Follow-up!

Most people give up just when they're about to achieve success.
They quit on the one yard line. They give up at the last minute
of the game, one foot from a winning touchdown.

—Ross Perot

Some network marketers get close to success and then give up. The problem is that we never know how close we are to success. We have to keep going to find out. The only thing that's certain is that giving up will *not* get us there. We must have patience and be willing to sacrifice some things now that will pay huge dividends in the future. Those who are successful just don't give up!

Here's a great mantra to repeat when you feel like quitting: *I will do today what others will not do, so tomorrow I can do what others cannot do.*

Follow-up is so important to success in network marketing. I believe that lack of follow-up is one of the biggest reasons why the statistics report such a large percentage of people who never make any money in a network marketing business. The vast majority quit working their business because they don't have the patience required. One of the things I find in common with other top income earners in my company is that we have an effective process for following up and staying in touch with our prospects.

We invite people to look at what we have to offer, and we make our presentations. When the prospect is not ready to make a decision, some network marketers give up, leaving business on the table. Then they wonder why they are not attracting any customers or business builders! Timing is everything. Just because someone is not ready today does not mean that they will not be ready to buy your products or join your team in the future. Circumstances and motivations change over time. Staying in touch and following up is essential.

If someone started a traditional business, they would expect to work hard for at least a couple of years before seeing any profit, and that's after investing hundreds of thousands of dollars and a lot of "sweat equity" to get the business up and running. Many people starting a network marketing business do not expect to invest much up-front time before reaping the rewards.

> *Perseverance separates the successful*
> *entrepreneurs from the non-successful ones.*
>
> *—Steve Jobs*

With consistent action—including regular follow-up—network marketers can work part-time (ten to fifteen hours a week) and build a significant passive income in two to five years. Sometimes it takes weeks or months before income is generated, and sometimes income starts flowing right away. Regardless of how long it takes to start generating a positive cash flow, the vast majority of prospects require at least some follow-up. Just as it is with traditional businesses, some network marketing prospects require months or even years of follow-up before they start using the products or enroll as a distributor.

The top income earners in any network marketing company will tell you that follow-up is a crucial part of their business success. The key is to keep any process you use *simple* and *duplicable*.

Here are some startling statistics that emphasize the importance of follow-up:

- Forty-eight percent of sales people never follow up with a prospect.
- Twenty-five percent of sales people make a second contact and then stop.
- Twelve percent of sales people only make three contacts and then stop.
- Only ten percent of sales people make more than three contacts.
- Eighty percent of sales are made on the fifth to twelfth contact.

Some network marketing companies provide a contact management system to their distributors. If your company does not, you will need to select a system that works best for you. Some people prefer paper systems, like a tickler file or a twelve-month file index system, and some prefer an electronic system such as Microsoft Outlook, ACT!, or Oprius (a software program created specifically

KATHY PAAUW

for network marketers). You may need to experiment a bit to find which system works best for you.

Multiple contacts with a prospect are important. However, a "contact" is not necessarily a sales call or a "pitch" for something you want someone else to buy or join. Some of the most powerful contacts include reaching out to let someone know that you are thinking about them and that you care, with no mention of business. This may be in the form of a card, e-mail, phone call, or personal visit.

Don't become the person that others avoid because all you talk about is your "opportunity." If people are crossing over to the other side of the road when they see you coming, chances are that you have fallen into this trap. Remember that people do business with people they know, like, trust, and remember. Be remembered as someone who cares about others. A business relationship will eventually evolve if it's meant to be. If it doesn't, you have still developed a friendship.

The benefit of using an electronic contact management system is that you can easily manipulate the data when you want to do lookups by different criteria. If you use an Internet-based contact management system, you have access to your data from anywhere in the world.

I will share a process that I am using for managing all the action steps I take with my prospects, customers, and team members. If the terminology below does not fit your company's process, make adjustments so it works for you.

Step 1: Create the following groups in your contact manager to help you manage the stages that each prospective customer or distributor moves through. If your contact manager alphabetizes the names of your groups, include the numbers as part of the group name, as I have demonstrated below:

1-Invite

2-Present

3-Follow Up

4-Train

Step 2: Add each contact to the appropriate group.

1. *Invite* is for all the people you want to share your company offerings with (your warm market list) but whom you have not yet invited to take a look.

2. *Present* is for people who are ready to learn more about your company offerings by watching a video, experiencing a product demonstration, or whatever process you use.

3. *Follow Up* is for the people who have participated in a presentation and have not yet become a customer or distributor. You may need to follow up with them many times before they are ready to enroll. This is the weakest part of the process for most network marketing professionals.

4. *Train* is for the people who have already been enrolled as a customer or distributor and need training on how to use your product/service or how to build a team.

Step 3: Use notes and reminders

By keeping notes, you will have more detailed information about each person and will remember when and why you want to follow up with them. When you follow up, enter a note in your contact manager so you have a history of your follow-ups. Keep track of their hobbies, interests, what they like about your offerings, what their concerns were, etc.

By scheduling reminders in your contact manager, you will be reminded about what to do and when to do it. You can schedule reminders for making follow-up calls, scheduling appointments, or sending e-mails, cards, or informational materials.

Step 4: Use your new system and keep it up-to-date

When you are working on your daily business-building activities, if you are using an electronic contact management system, do a search for whatever group you want to focus on that day. For example, you can do a search for the "Invite" group and determine who you will make introductions to

                    KATHY PAAUW

today. Once you've done this, you will remove them from the "Invite" group and add them to the "Present" group. Your next action is to schedule a presentation with them. Once you complete a presentation, you remove them from "Present" and add them to the "Follow Up" group. Once they get started as a customer or distributor, you move them into the "Train" group so you can track who needs to be trained.

Other groups to consider creating in your contact manager

This will help you track the interest level of your prospects:

- *Prospect—Hot*: those who express a strong interest and say they want to sign up but haven't yet.

- *Prospect—Not Interested*: people who said that your offering is not for them. Stay in touch with this group by occasionally connecting with them via phone, e-mail, bump-into, a card, or letter campaign (can be set up at whatever interval you wish—monthly, quarterly, semiannually, etc.). Even if what you have to offer is not for them, you may get referrals for others they think of who would benefit. Also, people's needs change over time. Just because they are not interested today does not mean they will never be interested. If you don't keep in touch, there is very little chance you will ever know if they change their mind.

- *Prospect—Not Now*: they may be interested at some point in the future, but not right now. Stay in touch with this group by occasionally connecting with them via phone, e-mail, bump-into, or a card campaign (can be set up at whatever interval you wish—monthly, quarterly, semiannually, etc.). Their needs and circumstances will change over time. Just because they are not ready today does not mean they will not be ready tomorrow. If your offerings fall off their radar, they may never enroll, or someone else might sponsor them when they are ready.

- *Prospect—Need More Time*: those who express interest but need more time before they decide.

- *Specialty Groups* may be created for people who belong to a particular profession, have a special interest in a specific offering you have, etc.

A prospect may be in more than one group. For example, someone may be in your "Follow Up" group and your "Prospect-Hot" group. This gives you the ability to do a more detailed search for those who meet multiple criteria.

Although this may seem complex to someone just getting started, over time you will have hundreds (even thousands) of people in various stages of the process. Without a system in place, it becomes nearly impossible to manage it all. Setting up a system like this when you are getting started will save you lots of time and frustration later on.

When most people think of follow-up, they think of doing so with prospects. There is one other very important kind of follow-up, and that's with your existing distributors. In Randy Gage's book *Making the First Circle Work: The Foundation for Duplication in Network Marketing*, he teaches you the difference between what you really control and what you can only influence by creating a culture that causes true duplication. One of my favorite techniques he shares is finding someone in your organization who shows a "spark" no matter what level they are on.

> *Someone qualifies as sparking by sponsoring a lot of people or showing volume growth. When you see a spark, feed the fire by pouring gasoline on it! You do this by getting in touch and letting those people know you are willing to travel to their town and do some presentations and training for them. Of course, this excites them, but it also moves that excitement all through the sponsorship line above them. Make sure you are in touch with the leaders above and keep them abreast of what is going on beneath them. So the lower down you work, the better results you create.*

> *—Randy Gage, Making the First Circle Work*

This same follow-up technique can be used to promote events. Events are the lifeblood of building a network marketing business. They keep people connected, excited, and positive. You cannot just announce events and expect that your team will register. You need to promote events. Begin by being the first to register. Then work farther down in the line of your organization, getting them to register for the next major event. Once you've done this, call the person above them and say, "You have five people registered for the xxxx event. Have you gotten your tickets yet?" Once that person has registered, go up the line to the next level. Repeat this all the way up the line. Before you know it, you'll have a lot of people registered who would not have otherwise attended the event.

                    KATHY PAAUW

FREEDOM CHALLENGE

If you do not have a contact management system set up, select one and begin using it. Below are some tips:

- This can be paper or electronic. Choose something you can consistently use and maintain.
- If you are using an electronic contact management system, create groups.
- Add notes to your contact records.
- Add follow-up reminders to your calendar.
- Set up a reminder system to check your team reports at least monthly to see who is sparking. Carve out time in your schedule to follow up with a personal phone call to these people.

CHAPTER 10

Managing Paper and Information

I use a simple decision-making process that has helped me and many of my clients to manage paper, e-mail, and other information. I learned this process from Chris Crouch, author of *Getting Organized,* and he has given me permission to share this process with you.

Chris has identified *five ways* that things come into our busy lives these days:

1. *Paper*

2. *E-mail*

3. *Voice Mail / text messages*

4. *Verbal requests*

5. *Thoughts in your head* (things to do)

To keep this simple, you'll need to gather all five types of incoming items together in one place. I suggest containing it all in an inbox until you have time to make one of these five decisions. Empty your inbox daily. Once you take something out of your inbox, you *never* put it back in there. Instead, you make one of five decisions, as I will demonstrate below.

You can put paper and even printed e-mails in your inbox. Write down voice mail messages, verbal requests, and thoughts in your head on a 3" × 5" index card and place those in your inbox too. Be sure you only put *one message or one task or idea on each index card.* Then begin to filter through the contents of your inbox one item at a time. Give your full attention to the item in front of you.

Chris has also identified *five decisions* that need to be made for each item that comes into your life (in one of the five forms mentioned above):

1. *Discard:* toss, recycle, shred, delete (if electronic).

2. *Delegate:* give it to someone else to handle.

3. *Take immediate action:* do it now!

4. *File for follow-up* (tickler file): Set up a tickler file system that has tabs for one to thirty-one (days of the current month) and also tabs for all twelve months of the year. I like the Smead daily/monthly desk file/sorter (Smead UPC code 89235), which contains a total of forty-three dividers. Place the item in the dated file for when you intend to take the *next* action. You must check your tickler file each day in order for this to work effectively.

5. *File for future reference:* I suggest that you set up a filing system that enables you to cross-reference the contents by not only the file name but also some key words associated with the file. The number one reason people pile instead of file is a fear of never finding it again because they cannot remember what they called the file. There are several programs available that will provide the ability for you to do a keyword search and find the location (file number) of the item you are looking for.

Consider the above decisions in the order suggested. Think of a funnel. Everything enters the top of the funnel, and the volume of paper or electronic information gets smaller as you move down the funnel.

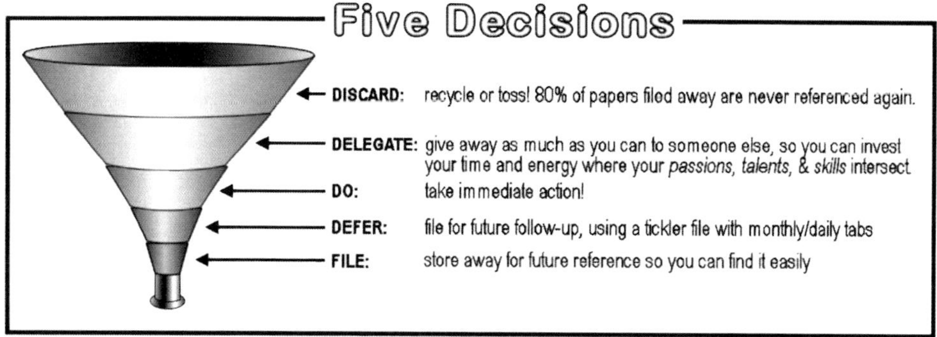

If you can throw it away, you won't need to consider the other four options. If you can give it away (delegate it), you won't need to consider the other three options. If it requires immediate action, you won't need to file it away for future follow-up (tickler file) or reference (filing system).

Several years ago, I coached a client who had been through some major life experiences, including domestic abuse and eventually a divorce. My client wanted some life coaching as well as some assistance with organizing her environment, time, and her life. She was starting fresh and was not sure where to begin. At one point, she was preparing for a move to a much smaller home, and she needed to get rid of a lot of things. We talked about what was weighing her down and what she was ready to let go of. I taught her the five-decision process. Several days later, I received this e-mail from her:

> Kathy,
>
> I have been going through stuff all day since we talked on the phone—sorting, boxing, chucking, etc. I went through some things I had saved for sentimental reasons, and I was really able to enjoy them and then say, "Okay, it's time to get rid of these now."
>
> When I went to get ready for bed, I looked in the mirror, and something amazing took place. I *saw myself* standing there. I have not done that for a long time.
>
> Every time I have looked in the mirror, for as long as I can remember, I have noticed how lost I've looked. I know that's not a great thought, but I honestly thought it anyway. It was *so wonderful* to see the *real me* standing there. The thing that caught my attention was that my eyes were sparkling! Yep, they were, and I smiled so big! *Hello me*!! :o)
>
> Maybe when I get all this moving over with and get settled I will find *all* of me! I really do *miss me*!!!
>
> Love, hugs, and a big sparkly smile!
> (shared anonymously with permission)

When we let go of things that weigh us down, we make room for new things to appear in our lives! This client made room in her life for a new relationship and is now happily remarried.

As my colleague Barbara Hemphill says, "Clutter is postponed decisions." Imagine the possibilities when you are clear enough about your priorities that you can make decisions right now about what to do with paper and information as it comes in—toss it, delegate it, do it now, do it later (and when), or file away for future reference.

Letting go is one of the hardest things for some people to do. Since 80 percent of what we file or store is never referenced or used again, here's a list of trigger questions that will help you decide what to keep and what to let go of:

1. What's the worst thing that could happen if I got rid of this?

2. By the time I *might* need this, will it be obsolete?

3. If I got rid of this and discovered I needed it later, could I fairly easily replace it?

4. If my office/home burned down, would I actively work to replace this item?

5. Does it have tax or legal implications?

6. How will keeping this enhance my life? (Before answering this question, consider my definition of clutter—see below.)

Clutter: anything you *own, possess,* or *do* that does not enhance your life on a *regular* basis.

My definition of "clutter" goes far beyond the tangible items in your physical environment. Clutter can be *thoughts, activities,* and even *relationships* in your life.

You are the only one who can determine what a "regular basis" is. For example, if you were to be audited on your tax returns from three years ago, it would definitely enhance your life to have kept the supporting documents to defend any tax deductions you declared since the government can audit you for a tax return you filed three years ago. If you use holiday decorations once a year, this would be considered a "regular basis"; but if you have not used that decoration for several years, it may be time to give it away to someone else who could make better use of it.

Sometimes *activities, relationships,* and *thoughts* get expressed in the form of physical clutter. Here's an example of how that works.

I know someone who inherited an entire household of furnishings that he really disliked. The furnishings simply did not fit his style or personality. His belief (thought) was that he had to keep it all because these things once belonged to his mother, and she had left all her earthly possessions to him. He disliked the furnishings so much that he avoided spending time in his own home. Once he let go of the belief that he would be a "bad person" if he did not keep everything that had once belonged to his beloved mother, he was able to find other people who could put these furnishings to good use. Once he made this decision, he furnished his home in a way that inspires him, and he now enjoys spending time there.

FREEDOM CHALLENGE

Set up an effective system to help you process paper and information as it comes into your life:

- Create a stacking tray labeled INCOMING to gather paper and information until you have time to process it. Create another tray labeled TO FILE for papers that do not require action and simply need to be filed away for future reference.

- Set up a tickler file system with tabs for January-December and 1-31 (for the current month). If you are not familiar with what this is, I invite you to participate in my free monthly webinar, Buried in Paper, where you will learn how to set up an effective paper and information management process that includes a tickler file system.

 KATHY PAAUW

- Process information from your INCOMING tray once a day, using the five-decision process outlined in this chapter. At the end of each day this tray should be completely empty.

Define what's cluttering up your life. (Hint: All these work off each other.)

- *tangible items* that do not enhance your life on a regular basis
- *thoughts* that do not enhance your life on a regular basis
- *activities* that do not enhance your life on a regular basis
- *relationships* that do not enhance your life on a regular basis

As you change habits, you may benefit from having a reminder of the questions to ask yourself when deciding whether to keep or toss something. Visit *www. TheMusicOfYourHeart.com/declutter* to request a free postcard that lists the trigger questions mentioned above. When it arrives in the mail, post the questions in a place where you will see them daily.

CHAPTER 11

Accountability Partnerships

Once you've identified your values, vision, and goals, it's time to take committed action.

One of the most powerful support tools you can create for yourself is an accountability partnership. I have been working with my accountability partner for a few years, and this process has made a huge difference in what I've accomplished. Both my partner and I are committed to the process. That's what makes it work!

I propose four components to your support structure:

1. A daily check-in via e-mail with your accountability partner, Monday-Friday, as well as at least one phone conversation weekly. I will outline how that works later in this chapter.

2. Share your intentions (see end of chapter 1) and SMART goals (see end of this chapter) with your accountability partner so he/she can better support you.

3. If you have any measuring tools you use for your business, share your daily results with your partner. For example, I have a "Daily 8 Scorecard" I use to track eight specific activities that top income earners in our company repeat consistently. I share my daily score with my partner. If you have specific daily activities or habits that you track, you can share these with your accountability partner.

4. If you want help keeping your focus on gratitude, share with your partner at least one thing you are grateful for every day. Even if you had a bad day, you can always find something to be grateful for.

Accountability Process

An accountability process is simply sharing with another person (an accountability partner) your intentions or goals and then regularly reporting your results regardless of whether or not you've been successful at achieving them. Jim Bunch, an ultimate life coach I worked with in 2008, taught me how to play the Happy-Healthy-Wealthy game, which I have incorporated into my accountability process.

One of the things I love about the Happy-Healthy-Wealthy game is that it provides balance in my life—a very important part of success. Why strive for creating wealth if we forfeit happiness and health in the process? You determine what defines these three areas for yourself.

Here's how it works. My accountability partner and I create happy, healthy, and wealthy goals or intentions for the next workday. We e-mail each other each workday evening, reporting our results from today and our intentions for tomorrow.

Below is an example of an e-mail I sent to my accountability partner. Notice that it is simple and short. In this example, I sent this on the eve of January 4, reporting my results for what actually happened that day as well as my intentions for the next day, January 5.

SUBJECT: KP 1/5/10 Goals

1/4/10 Report:
Happy: Dinner with my friend, Liz—DONE
Healthy: Workout with Personal Trainer—DONE
Wealthy: 2 mentoring calls—DONE, 1 prospect call—NOT DONE
Daily 8 Score: 9/8 (means that I earned 9 points and had a goal of 8)
Grateful for the wonderful family vacation we just had in Mexico.

1/5/10 Goals:
Happy: Get a massage
Healthy: Treadmill for 45 minutes
Wealthy: Half day planning session to finalize 90-day plan
Daily 8 Goal: 8

Tips to Ensure a Successful Accountability Partnership:

- Selection of accountability partner: this should *not* be someone you are intimately close to, like a spouse. Your partner needs to be someone who will call you on things (hold you accountable) if you are not keeping your commitments to yourself without being judgmental or punitive in their approach.

- Suspend judgment! If your partner cannot suspend judgment, get a different partner. When someone is judging you, your focus will be on getting angry with them for judging you, rather than on looking inward and deepening the learning about what's stopping you from keeping your commitments to yourself. Here's an example of the difference:

    Being in judgment: "What's wrong with you? Are you getting lazy? You keep telling me that you're going to follow up with that prospect and you haven't done it!" (The word "you" is typically used a lot with judgmental comments. This puts the other person on the defense rather than encouraging them to be introspective.)

    Holding accountability: "I notice that you've been saying that you are going to follow up with that prospect who is on your 'chicken list,' and for the last several days, you've reported that you have not done it. What's stopping you?" (Use "I" statements to report what you notice. Ask questions to help your partner deepen their learning.)

- Write down intentions that are most important to you. In other words, if you do nothing else, you are committing to doing these things. Do not create a long list of intentions in each category as that will sabotage your efforts. You may have more than one intention for each category as long as you keep it realistic. Typically, you will do more than what you committed to in your e-mail to your partner.

- Set your goals or intentions the day or evening before so you can begin the next day with clarity. If you find that there are certain important activities you keep avoiding, plan to do them before noon.

- List at least one intention in the areas of happiness, health, and wealth. This is a *whole life* process, not just about building your business. If you have other important goals or intentions, include them here. For example, if you have a job or another business, you can include them. Some people find that the "happy" intention is the hardest one to identify. Even if it is something small, be sure you identify one intention for each of these three areas.

- Once a week, ask yourself these questions and share your responses with your partner. This will help you evaluate your activities—including how you are *being* and not just what you are *doing*—to see how your habits and behaviors are working for you:

    - What do I want to *start?*
    - What do I want to *stop?*
    - What do I want to *continue?*

- This is not a place to list reasons or excuses to shame, blame, or justify. If you do not follow through, simply write "Not done."

I suggest that you have an initial conversation to discuss how you want to structure your relationship and to provide whatever personal and professional information you choose to share with each other.

My accountability partner and I have a call at least once a week to talk about what is working, what is not, and how we can support each other. Decide what will best support your partnership. If one of you does not receive an e-mail, be sure that you e-mail or call to check in and let your partner know that you missed receiving it.

This process will only work if you are consistent and if you keep it short and simple so it does not take over your life. If your partner is not consistently participating in this accountability process, get a new partner.

Even if your accountability partner is away on vacation or unable to read what you sent, *the power is in writing down and sending your intentions.* This is true for a couple reasons: (1) Doing this facilitates you declaring your goals before the start of the day so you are clear about what to do; (2) By telling someone else your intentions and then reporting whether or not you did what you said you'd do, you are much more likely to follow through. I've occasionally found myself on the treadmill late at night before I e-mail my partner just so I can say I did it!

This process only works if you are 100 percent honest with yourself and you don't weasel out on your commitments by making excuses about why you did not do something. It's also important that you send accurate reports to your accountability partner. You only cheat yourself when you are not 100 percent honest in your reporting.

We must all suffer one of two things:
the pain of discipline or the pain of regret or disappointment.

—Jim Rohn

FREEDOM CHALLENGE

- Select an accountability partner.

- Review the accountability check-in process and tips for best results.

- Identify your SMART (specific, measurable, attainable, relevant, time-bound) goals for the next ninety days in the areas of happiness, health, and wealth. Share these with your accountability partner.

- Send an email report of your goals or intentions to your partner daily, sharing your Happy-Healthy-Wealthy goals. List no more than three goals for each area—activities you intend to do tomorrow. You will most likely do other things, as well. These are activities you will definitely do tomorrow, no matter what.

    Happy goals: These goals are related to relationships, hobbies, family and free time, personal growth, or areas of life that bring greater happiness and fulfillment. Focus is both on what you are *doing* and on who you are *being* in the process.

    Goal 1:
    Goal 2:
    Goal 3:

Healthy goals: These goals are related to diet, exercise, hydration, rest and rejuvenation, stress reduction, appearance, and physical, mental, and spiritual health.

Goal 1:
Goal 2:
Goal 3:

Wealthy goals: These goals are related to income generation, investments/ leveraging your money, savings (college education, retirement, etc.), leaving a legacy through charitable giving or volunteer work, and your overall relationship with money.

Goal 1:
Goal 2:
Goal 3:

CHAPTER 12

Let Go of Your Attachments to the Outcome

Letting go of the attachment to an outcome is so important to your success with any goal. Those who let go of the attachment can still be focused on intention and ready to take necessary actions.

My friend and colleague, Robert MacPhee, has written a wonderful book, *Manifesting for Non Gurus: How to Quickly and Easily Attract Lasting Results*. In his book, he provides a list of six signs that help you determine if you have an attachment to the outcome of a situation:

1. Needing to know *how*
2. Needing something *now*
3. Hooking into the *judgments* of others
4. Hooking into your *own opinions* of others or yourself
5. Hooking into *guilt*
6. Hooking into *fear*

I'll provide some examples to help you relate to these six signs.

1. **Needing to know *how*.** There are so many ways that your intentions could manifest. If your self-talk is saying that you "should" do something a certain way or by a certain time, or that you should take a specific step in order to "get" what you want, you are attached. Perhaps you have a belief that you cannot start working on a goal until you have figured out *how* to do it. That belief stops many people from ever getting started.

Think of driving at night, when you can only see a couple hundred feet in front of you. You don't have to see the whole distance at once or know *how* to get from point A to point B. Even if you have a GPS system in your car, you may need to make adjustments because of construction or an accident. In other words, you cannot possibly know exactly *how* you will get there. As you are driving along, you can only focus on what you do *now*.

2. **Needing something *now*.** Being attached to having something right now is not very helpful. Think of a car salesman who really needs to make the sale today. Your experience with that person is vastly different when they focus on what's best for you rather than doing everything in their power to get their month-end bonus by making the sale today. Which approach will make you more likely to buy from them?

   Here's a piece of advice I give my team all the time: "Show, don't tell. Share, don't sell." It's about *showing* people how they can change or improve someone else's life, not about *selling* a product, service, or business opportunity.

   Timing is everything. I learned this lesson the hard way when I tried to push a prospect into signing up before the end of the month. I wanted to win an incentive award, and I needed one more person to sign up in that last twenty-four hours of the month. Although my prospect had told me he was planning to become a distributor on the ninth of the following month, I encouraged him to sign up that day. To this day, he still has not signed up. I believe it's because I was focused on what was best for *me* instead of what was best for *him*. I have vowed to never do that again.

3. **Hooking into the *judgments* of others.** There's nothing wrong with considering the advice and opinions of others. If you feel driven by their opinions, then you are hooked into what they think. If those you spend the most time with would not be supportive of your intentions, perhaps it is time to consider whom you invite into your inner circle. You become like the people you spend the most time with.

4. **Hooking into your *own opinions* of others or yourself.** If you spend a large portion of your time and energy focused on judging others or yourself, your attachment to these judgments will get in the way of you manifesting your intentions. This is a tremendous energy drain. I recently experienced this myself when I had a disagreement with the way someone decided to do something I was involved in. Rather than focusing on my own intentions, I kept my focus on my judgments about what the other person was doing "wrong." My judgments and my need to be right cost me about a week of productive work time.

    Here's a great technique for turning the tides when you catch your own self-defeating voice being active. Write yourself a letter about whatever topic is on your mind. There's only one rule. You can only write down what you've already accomplished or what you are capable of doing, not what your self-defeating voice would have to say about the topic or situation. Give your voice permission to be supportive, encouraging, positive, and caring.

5. **Hooking into *guilt*.** When our behavior does not match what we believe a good person would do, we feel guilty. To let go of the guilt, we must either change our behavior or change our beliefs about what it means to be a good person.

    For example, if you were raised with the belief that "money is the root of all evil," and that belief holds you back from doing what you know will create massive wealth, here are three possible options:

    *   Sabotage your efforts so you don't make so much money.
    *   Do your best to manage the guilt as your income goes up.
    *   Change your belief and recognize that money itself is not evil. It's when we sacrifice who we are *being* for the sake of *having* more that we get into trouble. We can also choose to do good or evil with the money we create.

6. **Hooking into *fear*.** When we are afraid, we set negative goals. We imagine what we don't want, and then we put all sorts of energy into tapping the emotions that accompany that fear. What you focus on, you get more of. In other words, you manifest exactly what you don't want. To overcome fear, tap into the emotion that accompanies what

                    KATHY PAAUW

you *do* want instead of focusing on the emotion that accompanies what you are afraid of.

If you fear failure, search for the emotion that accompanies your perception of success. By focusing on your intention, you'll establish a stronger connection to the feelings and emotions that will attract the results you desire.

The word "crisis" is written in Chinese with two famous characters: *danger* and *opportunity*—the yin and yang. When you are afraid to do something, ask yourself, "Is my fear based on protecting myself from *danger*, or am I experiencing fear of failure, which prevents me from seizing *opportunity*?"

Our attachment and need to control what someone else does (or doesn't do) can actually create resistance that prevents things from changing. As a parent, I recall many times when I wanted my daughter to do something. The more I focused on what I wanted her to do, the more resistant she became to doing it. My attachment (and the ensuing power struggles) actually fueled what I didn't want.

> *When we let go of attachments, we free up our attention for other more important uses and clear the channels through which we receive ideas, insights and intuition. The time and attention we were previously spending on thoughts, feelings and emotions that do not match who we are and do not support us in getting where we want to go, are now freed up. When our minds are filled with idle chatter, judgment, worry and fear, we cannot hear the most valuable ideas, insights, and intuitive messages. This is the power associated with letting go of attachments.*
>
> *—Robert MacPhee*

One way to determine if you are attached to the outcome is to ask yourself, "Am I giving to *give*, or am I giving to *get?*" If you'd like to do some deeper work on "letting go" of an attachment to the outcome, I encourage you to read Hale Dwoskin's book, *The Sedona Method*. I also recommend his powerful week-long workshops in Sedona, Arizona.

One of my favorite books is *The Go-Giver* by Bob Burg and John David Mann. In the book, the authors share five laws of stratospheric success:

1. *The law of value:* your true worth is determined by how much more you give in value than you take in payment.

2. *The law of compensation:* your income is determined by how many people you serve and how well you serve them.

3. *The law of influence:* your influence is determined by how abundantly you place other people's interests first.

4. *The law of authenticity:* the most valuable gift you have to offer is yourself.

5. *The law of reciprocity:* The key to effective giving is to stay open to receiving.

If you are attached to the outcome, you may feel desperate to get the result you desire. That desperation will drive people away. It's also hard to be creative when you're feeling desperate, so it's more difficult to think outside the box or to find ways to contribute your authentic talents and skills. When you are attached to a specific outcome, you may not be open to receiving a gift when it arrives in a different form than you were expecting. All five of the laws above are so powerful, and they all relate to the topic of letting go.

From time to time, I receive calls or e-mails from network marketers who want to know my secret to success as a top income earner in my company. I recently received a phone call from someone who has been involved in our company for a year and has not experienced the success she was hoping for. She was calling to ask what my secret was to success. Here's what I shared with her.

There are no secrets. Everything I do I have shared in my training calls and e-mails that are available to everyone in our company. Building a network marketing business is like working on a farm. Here are the steps required:

- We *begin with fertile soil.* If the soil is not rich in nutrients, the plants will not flourish. In network marketing, the nutrients are represented by the foundational work necessary to launch a successful business. We add nutrients to the soil by doing our own *personal development work* and by *building relationships.*

- Next we *plant the seeds*. We *invite* people to look at what we have to offer, and then we *present* it to them. These are two separate steps. Some people try to cut corners and combine the two, and that generally does not work. Keep the invitation and the presentation separate.

- Then we consistently *fertilize and water the seeds* even before we can see the sprouts pop through the surface of the ground. This is part of a *follow-up* process that is usually necessary since many people do not make an immediate decision. Follow-up is one of the weakest areas for many network marketers.

  Some plants grow very rapidly, and others take time to germinate. Did you know that if certain plant species do not lie dormant during the winter months, the plant begins to die? Some of our prospects will lie dormant (timing is everything), and if we do not follow up when they're ready to "sprout," we may lose them.

- Sometimes *weeding* is necessary so the unproductive growth does not crowd out the plants we want to keep. In network marketing, we call this *sorting*. We sort the prospects who express interest and are motivated to work (our "aces") from those who are not. We also sort those whom we like and trust from those we do not choose to spend time with. We do our best *not* to apply fertilizer on the weeds. Occasionally, we have difficulty deciphering the difference between a weed and a plant, and we may unintentionally fertilize it for a while.

- Eventually we *reap the harvest*. We *sign up* a new customer or distributor and do whatever *training* is necessary to enjoy the fruits of our labor.

- The *life cycle starts over* as we take the seeds from a new plant and place them in the ground, preferably in fertile soil. In network marketing, this is called *duplication*.

There are several essential ingredients required to enjoy a successful harvest: *duplicating specific activities consistently over time,* and *letting go of the attachment to the outcome.* As on a farm, you cannot fertilize and water the plants *when you feel like it*, putting off these tasks when you are not in the mood. Doing the above things *consistently* will yield a harvest. You also cannot have an *attachment* to how much time it will take to see the fruits of your labor, or which seeds in the ground will never sprout and which will bring a great harvest. Nature does not take shortcuts, and it does not provide instant results. Do your best to consistently fertilize and water your crop, and then *allow* nature to take its course.

As you think of the steps mentioned above, consider where you need to let go of your attachment to the outcome. If it's not working as nature intended it to, go back to step one and look at the foundation upon which you are building your business. You can never do too much *personal development work* or build too many *quality relationships*!

Discipline yourself to do the things you need to do when you need to do them, and the day will come when you will be able to do the things you want to do when you want to do them!

—*Zig Ziglar*

FREEDOM CHALLENGE

Determine how you are "attached" to the outcome of intentions that are important to you:

- needing to know *how*
- needing something *now*
- hooking into the *judgments* of others
- hooking into your *own opinions* of others or yourself
- hooking into *guilt*
- hooking into *fear*

Identify a situation where you have an attachment to the outcome. Now describe a response (action, thought, etc.) that will help you let go of your attachment to the outcome.

KATHY PAAUW

Here are some questions to ask yourself as related to the five laws of stratospheric success:

1. How can you give away more value than you receive in payment?

2. How can you serve more people? How can you serve them better than you are now?

3. How can you place the interest of others above your own?

4. How can you more authentically show up? What gifts do you have to offer that you are not currently tapping into?

5. How can you make yourself more open to receiving what is already being offered?

If you are not "reaping the harvest" you desire, which part of the process needs more attention?

- Are you working with fertile soil—doing personal development work and building relationships?
- Are you planting enough seeds—inviting and presenting?
- Are you fertilizing and watering consistently—following up?
- Are you weeding out the unproductive growth—sorting?
- Are you reaping the harvest—signing up and training?
- Are you repeating the life cycle—promoting duplication on your team?

CHAPTER 13

Who Owns the Problem?

Part of letting go of attachments is to identify who owns the problem. I learned this valuable lesson when our daughter was about four years old.

My husband and I were taking a parenting class, and we had mentioned a parenting challenge to our instructor to seek his advice. Here was the challenge: we both worked full-time and needed to get our daughter to day care early so we could be at work on time. We knew that she could dress herself, but she refused to do it—a tactic she most likely was using to get more of our attention.

We asked our instructor what to do. He replied with a question for us: "Who owns the problem?" I responded by saying that I did because if she did not get dressed, I would be late to work. He asked me, "Why do *you* own the problem?" and I repeated my response in an exasperated tone: "Because if she doesn't get dressed, I will be late to work!" The instructor said, "I still don't understand why *her* not getting dressed is *your* problem!"

I didn't understand what the instructor was trying to say until he hit me over the head with his advice: "Why don't you just take your daughter to day care—*however she is dressed*—when it's time to go?" I said, "You mean . . . stick her in the car in *just her underwear in January*, when it's so cold outside?" He suggested that I try it.

The next morning, I gave our daughter the fifteen-minute, ten-minute, and five-minute warnings that we would be leaving. When it was time to go, I said, "Okay, time to go! Let's get in the car!" She protested that she was not ready, and I took her out to the car in her underwear, strapped her seat belt around her, and placed a bag of clothes next to her. By the time we got to day care, she had managed to completely dress herself, with her seat belt still on!

The following morning she was dressed and ready to go when it was time to leave. Apparently, once our daughter owned the problem, she was motivated to solve it! It was never an issue again.

Stephen Covey shares a wonderful model in his book *The Seven Habits of Highly Effective People*. We all have a *circle of concern* and a *circle of influence*.

Here's an example of how this works. Let's say I have placed world hunger in my circle of concern. I could work the rest of my life to stamp out world hunger, but doing so is beyond my individual grasp. When I keep my focus on what I *cannot* do, I get frustrated and discouraged. What can I do about world hunger? There are thousands of things I can do. Here are two ideas: (1) I can make contributions to organizations like World Vision, Kiva, or Heifer International, which help people become self-reliant by getting an education and gaining the ability to support themselves and (2) I can choose to make my purchases from Fair Trade organizations that pay fair wages, provide safe working conditions and long-term, stable business partnerships for disadvantaged artisans and producers.

When I focus on what I *can* do, my circle of influence grows and the circle of concern diminishes.

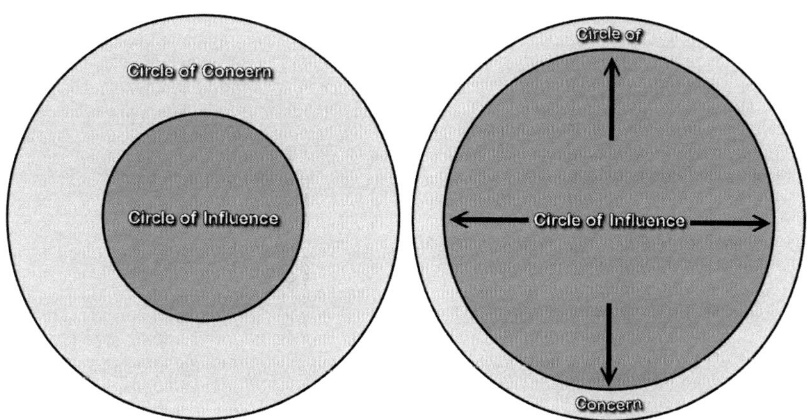

Think of ways to be more proactive with the things you *can* do something about. Putting focus on what you don't want is disempowering. Focusing on what you can *do* is proactive and empowering. Covey suggests, "Be part of the solution, not part of the problem."

When you have distributors on your team who are not doing what you want them to do or what they say they are going to do, ask yourself, "Who owns the problem?" If you own the problem, they will not be motivated to solve it. Allow your team members to own their own problems. Give them support without rescuing.

Managers light a fire under people; leaders light a fire in people.

—Kathy Austin, management consultant

Fall in love with helping people discover their own creative genius! Your job is to believe in your team members even before they believe in themselves. See their potential and be ready to work with them when they are ready.

One of my top team leaders contacted me in total frustration. She had a distributor who kept talking like she was going to do big things, but she was not taking the action necessary to produce any of the results she had committed to. It was clear to me who owned the problem, and her team member was happy to let her team leader "own" it for her.

Here was my advice: You can lead a horse to water, but you can't make it drink. If your horse does not want to drink, go find some thirsty horses!

How often have you invested time, thought, and energy into "helping" those who are not ready to take action? If you've already sponsored several people into your organization, you know that some will not do anything after they enroll. Timing is everything. I have someone on my team who became a distributor several years ago and did nothing. I kept in touch with her over the years, and last year her circumstances had changed, and she was ready to get going. She has been on fire ever since.

Although my support is always available to everyone on my team, until a team member is internally motivated to take action, there's not much I can do. I keep inviting them to the watering hole; they have to be thirsty enough to drink.

Bill Britt, one of the most successful distributors in an established network marketing company, shared the business opportunity with 1,200 people; nine hundred said no and only three hundred signed up. Out of those three hundred, only eighty-five did something and thirty-five of them worked the business seriously. Out of those thirty-five serious business builders, eleven distributors made him a millionaire. It's a numbers game. Britt achieved his success because he kept his focus on the thirsty horses in his pack, and he was able to let go of any attachment to the rest.

If you are a new network marketing professional and have access to great support from your sponsor or upline, count your blessings. If you do not have great immediate upline support, that's no excuse for your failure. If you want to succeed, you will find a way. Some of the top producers in my company—myself included—had very little support from their direct sponsor. If you look for assistance and ask for it, there are plenty of successful people who are eager to mentor you as long as you are committed to your own success as well as committed to helping others along the way.

One of the things I love most about network marketing is that our business model promotes a win-win atmosphere. In order to achieve personal career success and experience a prosperous life, you must help others to do the same. By sharing with others the principles that have enabled you to be personally successful, you have the opportunity to be part of creating global success.

One of the most beautiful compensations in life is that
no man can help another without helping himself.

—Ralph Waldo Emerson

FREEDOM CHALLENGE

Identify situations in your *personal* and *business/work life* where you currently "own" a problem that really belongs to someone else. What will you do (or not do) in order to allow the other person to own their problem?

Identify specific actions or choices you can take that will expand your circle of influence while shrinking your circle of concern.

PART FOUR

Be the Path to Freedom

CHAPTER 14

Network Marketing Provides a Clear Path to Freedom

What most people need is an avenue to create passive income . . . We found that one business model stood out from the rest. This particular business model creates passive income, but requires relatively little cash investment to start up. It has very low overhead, and can be operated on a flexible part-time basis until it generates enough cash flow for the entrepreneur to transition out of his current full-time job. The business model is called network marketing.

—Robert Kiyosaki, *The Business of the 21st Century*

In chapter 1, I reviewed the many reasons why this is such a great time to be a network marketing professional.

Another benefit of running your own business is that you have the freedom to design your schedule and your activities according to what makes your heart sing. For those who are accustomed to having a boss tell you what to do, you may be uncomfortable with this newfound freedom at first. You may even find comfort in having someone else tell you what to do and how to do it. To a certain degree, the "what" and "how" of running your business is built into the network marketing model and is what makes our work duplicable. However, within this model, you will also find incredible freedom and flexibility.

It's tempting to look at what someone else in your company is doing with great success and try to emulate them, only to find that you hate what you're doing. Yes, do follow the basics that your company provides, *and* give yourself the freedom to put your own spin on how you show up and serve. It's a lot more fun when you tap into your own natural strengths, gifts, and talents. When you do that, it doesn't even feel like work! Oscar Wilde expressed it best: "Be yourself. Everyone else is already taken."

Microsoft cofounder Bill Gates delivered the commencement address at Harvard University in 2007 when he received an honorary degree. In his address, he said, "I hope you will judge yourselves, not on your professional accomplishments alone but also on how well you have addressed the world's deepest inequities . . . on how well you treated people a world away who have nothing in common with you but their humanity."

Network marketing offers a vehicle for creating lifestyle and financial freedom for yourself while transforming other people's lives and communities and raising global consciousness. All people of the world are connected. The Internet has enabled us to build business relationships and work globally without leaving our home offices. As you support others to believe in themselves, take action, and pursue their dreams, you are giving them the gift of hope. They, in turn, will do the same.

You deserve to enjoy lifestyle freedom right now—regardless of your current financial circumstances—while enjoying the journey along the way to financial freedom. You owe it to yourself to fight through the mental clutter of doubt, fear, and past challenges and plug into your own creative genius and untapped potential as you take action that will move you from where you are to where you want to be.

Ultimately, it does not matter how much wealth or power we have gained. What matters is how we have loved others and how we have improved the lives of humanity—how we have made a difference and left a legacy that will live on even after we are gone. Imagine a world where every man, woman, and child has all their basic needs met while building successful businesses that are based on servant leadership, love, cooperation, and mutual respect. We have an incredible opportunity to be part of changing humanity. We provide the path to freedom!

My boldest dream is to free millions of people from a life of limitation, helping them to achieve financial and lifestyle freedom while sharing their gifts and talents in a way that makes their heart sing.

Be the change you wish to see in the world.

—Gandhi

FREEDOM CHALLENGE

Write down three things you learned from reading this book. List at least one action step you will take for each, and by when, in order to put each new learning into practice.

One of the highest compliments a writer is blessed is to receive is feedback from those who have invested their time and resources to positively change their own life as a result of something they've learned from a book. I invite you to post your comments, stories, and insights at *www.TheMusicOfYourHeart.com*. I look forward to hearing from you!

CHAPTER 15

Compose the Song That Makes Your Heart Sing

The biggest tragedy is the waste of human resources.
The average person goes to his grave with his music still in him.

—Oliver Wendell Holmes

My wish for you is that the contents of this book have provided you with the following:

- clarity about your intentions and your bigger *why* that will keep you motivated, no matter what challenges you encounter;
- tools to help you "upgrade" your environments so you can create the ultimate lifestyle and financial freedom you desire; and
- planning, management, and accountability tools that will support you on your path to freedom.

Each chapter has some suggested Freedom Challenges that are designed to help you clarify, create, and support your path to freedom so you can live the life of your dreams and help others do the same.

To maximize your learning, I invite you to review the Freedom Challenges listed here and decide which ones you will complete. I also encourage you to put a note in your calendar to revisit these exercises annually. As you do more personal development work and grow as a professional in your business, your needs and responses will change. Downloading the Freedom Challenges will provide you with a clean copy to work from if you choose to complete these exercises each year.

To download the Freedom Challenges, visit TheMusicOfYourHeart.com. Click on Freedom Challenges and enter this password: *freedom*

This password is intended only for those who have had the experience of reading my book first. Many of the exercises will not make sense to someone who has not yet read it. Please invite others to read this book before accessing the Freedom Challenges.

I have recorded a song that conveys the core message of my book, and you can listen to it or download it at www.TheMusicOfYourHeart.com/song.

Chapter 1: Why Network Marketing? Page 25

—Create a realistic budget for your business expenses.
—Create a household budget and determine if you need a job to support you while growing your business.
—Devise a plan to eliminate debt.
—Devise a plan to put six months of savings away for you and your dependents to live off if needed.

Chapter 2: What is Your Intention? Page 33

—List fifty things you want to do, be, or have.
—Describe your perfect average day.

Chapter 3: Are You a Human *Being* or a Human *Doing*? Page 39

—Assess your work/life balance.
—If you are not currently living the life of your dreams, which of the five reasons do you most relate to?
—Define freedom for yourself.

Chapter 4: Affirmations—Lyrics to the Music of Your Heart Page 45

—Create your "I am . . ." statements and the *why* behind each one.
—Create a vision board that depicts exactly what you choose to attract into your life. Look at it daily.

LISTEN TO YOUR HEART

Lyrics by Kathy Wells Paauw and Kevin Cole
Music by Kevin Cole
Recorded by Fabsound Records
Replay at *www.TheMusicOfYourHeart.com/song*

In your life you can choose
So many songs to listen to.
But the one with all the power is inside of you.

Trust your heart,
Not your head.
Your heart will never steer you wrong.
Within your heart there is a song.
And it waits for you
And it wants for you...to

REFRAIN
Listen to your heart
And allow the part of you
That holds your dreams so near
To sing out loud and clear.

You'll hear the sweetest music
When you're who you're meant to be.
So listen to your heart.
Let it set you free.

Challenges will appear
And you may be so filled with fright.
Visualizing affirmations will turn dark to light.

Trust your heart,
Not your mind.
Your mind keeps telling you a lie
Of all the yesterdays gone by.
But your heart won't lie,
It knows the reason why.

REFRAIN
Listen to your heart
And allow the part of you
That holds your dreams so near
To sing out loud and clear.

You'll hear the sweetest music
When you're who you're meant to be.
So listen to your heart.
Let it set you free.

Take a moment.
Make a plan.
Be open to receive.

Trust yourself,
You know you can,
Move forward and believe!

REFRAIN
Listen to your heart
And allow the part of you
That holds your dreams so near
To sing out loud and clear.

You'll hear the sweetest music
When you're who you're meant to be.
So listen to your heart.
Listen to your heart.
Let it set you free.

©2011 Kevin Cole and Kathy Wells Paauw

     KATHY PAAUW

Listen to Your Heart
Is available for your listening pleasure

by visiting
www.TheMusicOfYourHeart.com/song

Personal Development

Jack Canfield
The Success Principles: How to Get from Where You Are to Where You Want to Be Key to Living Law of Attraction: A Simple Guide to Creating the Life of Your Dreams
Breakthrough to Success Workshop: http://www.canfieldtrainings.com/

Stephen R. Covey
First Things First
The Seven Habits of Highly Effective People
Mission Statement Builder: http://www.franklincovey.com/msb/

Bob Greene, Ann Kearney-Cooke
The Life You Want: Get Motivated, Lose Weight and Be Happy

Dr. Dean Ornish
Love and Survival

Robert Kiyosaki
The Business of the 21st Century

T. Harv Eker
Secrets of the Millionaire Mind

Jim Bunch
http://www.theultimategameoflife.com/

Vision Board Application
http://apps.facebook.com/ultimatevisionboard/index.php

Hale Dwoskin
The Sedona Method
http://www.sedona.com/

CoachVille LLC
The Nine Environments of You (originally created by Thomas Leonard)
www.coachville.com

Robert MacPhee
Manifesting for Non Gurus: How to Quickly and Easily Attract Lasting Results
http://manifestingfornongurus.com/about-us

Kody Bateman
Promptings: Your Inner Guide to Making a Difference
http://www.promptingsbook.com/

Marcus Buckingham and Donald Clifton
Now, Discover Your Strengths
http://www.strengthsfinder.com

Susan Jeffers
Feel the Fear and Do it Anyway
www.susanjeffers.com

Bob Burg and John David Mann
The Go-Giver
www.TheGoGiver.com/

Tony Rubleski
Mind Capture: How to Awaken Your Entrepreneurial Genius in a Time of Great Economic Change
www.MindCaptureBook.com

Network Marketing

Kody Bateman
MLM Blueprint (available in 2012)
www.EagleOnePublishing.com

Jordan Adler
Beach Money
www.BeachMoney.com

Judy O'Higgins, Kristi Lee, Karen Palmer
License to Dream: Every Woman's Guide to Financial Freedom through Network Marketing
www.license2dream.wordpress.com

Tommy Wyatt and Curtis Lewsey
Appreciation Marketing
www.AppreciationmMarketing.com/

Networking Times (published six times a year)
www.NetworkingTimes.com

Randy Gage
Making the First Circle Work: The Foundation for Duplication in Network Marketing
http://www.NetworkMarketingTimes.com

John Milton Fogg
The Greatest Networkers in the World: 21 ordinary people who became millionaires in Network Marketing and the true story of how they did it
http://thegreatestnetworkers.com

Kathy Paauw
www.TheMusicOfYourHeart.com
(check out Bonus page for free offerings)

Productivity

Barbara Hemphill
www.barbarahemphill.com/

Chris Crouch
Getting Organized
www.chriscrouch.typepad.com/

Kathy Paauw
Free tips, tools, and monthly newsletter: www.orgcoach.net

N

O

P

Q

R

S

T

U